OH, 108 AGAIN

Aging Gracefully by Living Fully in the 4th Quarter of Life

JAMES K. WAGNER

outskirts
press

TABLE OF CONTENTS

DEDICATION

*To all who desire to age gracefully
in the most challenging and rewarding
chapter of living...the fourth quarter*

FOREWORD

In this book, the author offers each reader some creative ways to ponder and intentionally develop three key concepts: aging gracefully, living fully, and the fourth quarter of life. In fifteen chapters, Jim Wagner shares in a personal, professional, and easy-to-comprehend manner questions that often surface in the minds of older adults. Here are a few of the chapter titles to whet your appetite: Soul and Spirituality; Solitude and Silence; Life After Life; Staying Healthy; Grace: God's Love in Action; Coping With Grief; Gratitude and Appreciation. There are over 65 resources listed for further pondering/learning/growing. In the presentation of the material itself, there are over 80 validating footnotes. What a wealth of holistic meaningful material! And, while the audience is targeted for older adults, I believe there is material here for any spiritual seeker, no matter what the age (whether it be chronological, biological, psychological, or spiritual age). The author has also provided Appendix A (Spiritual and Ethical Wellness Checklist) for each reader to examine their spirituality and identify potential areas for further "cultivated growth."

As one of many examples, chapter 7 on Life After Life could allay fears/misconceptions from the book's targeted audience. An overview of the life/death process and its meaning—from biblical references to current research on heaven, near-death experiences, and afterlife—is educational and spiritually uplifting. Living fully, as he explains very well, addresses all dimensions (physical, mental, emotional, spiritual) of aging. Some pertinent questions of essence are: "Are we paying attention to our soul and our relationship with our creator?" "What are some ways that I {you} can be more intentional, more aware, and more responsive to the spiritual dimensions of life?" "What are some ways to shape and develop my {your} spirituality and learn to live more gracefully?" On our spiritual journey, "are we transitioning beyond self-centered living into a more God-centered life?" Each chapter begins with a very relevant quote (from a wide variety of resources); followed by a leading question for the focus of that chapter; followed by a reflection. The author does an excellent job of developing and exploring the theme for each chapter. You will travel with the author as you witness each chapter develop and participate in the widening and deepening of that chapter's topical theme. At the end of each chapter there are four very thought-provoking "questions to ponder" to "close" the chapter. Here I would claim these four "questions to ponder" do much more than close the chapter; they take the material of that chapter—and prior chapters—and springboard to many new "opening ponderables." Sometimes they take the form of reflecting deeper; sometimes they become self-examination exercises; sometimes they are the springboard for meditative reflections. I could just imagine myself reading and absorbing this book and pondering the theme and questions in a small group setting!

While I have done many Bible studies in my last 50 years, chapter 4 (The Bible: Widely Purchased/Not Widely Read) is one of the best presentations on the Bible I have ever encountered, providing excellent overview, as well as attention to an effective "how to study the Bible." This chapter—as well as many of the other 15 chapters—helps to "provide moving beyond a self-centered living into God-centered life!" Later in the book the same thoroughness it overviewed and attention to detail are used again with prayer. As one of many examples on prayer (increased communication with creator), over a dozen descriptions/definitions of prayer and at least half a dozen great examples of types of prayer are presented. This "little" book is simply spiritually power packed! Most every topic developed is backed with meaningfully relevant Bible citations. The conception and creation of this book are scholarly yet also personal while being simultaneously broad and deep spiritually. Jim Wagner is a good initiator and developer of key thoughts. Borrowing from Bloom's Taxonomy of educational objectives, I would grade Jim no less than an A+ for his comprehension level, analytical level, and synthesis level questions/statements/reflections/resources.

As a prime example, chapter 5 on Salvation and Being Saved, provides good definitions, supplemented with easy-to-understand Greek and Hebrew resources, and with very on-target biblical references. Also included are testimonials from many people involved in the "senior" focus groups which provided meaningful and useful comments/perceptions/ideas for the inception and development of this priceless book for spiritual growth and understanding.

In chapter 10 on Grace: God's Love in Action, terms such as grace and love are defined, described, personalized, and then related and interrelated for a rich, holistic spiritual learning and growth experience. Throughout the book, the author shares from his mind, his spirit, his body, and his soul with many, many experiences. He relies on relevant and personal experience(s) of self, and of other "seniors" in the exploratory development for the ideas of this book. One of the many powerful personable spiritual examples is his description of his monastery stay and the ensuing many reflections that aided the development of his "perception/conception" of an evolving life of prayer. Also, this creative publication contains a super wealth of outstanding (scholarly and spiritually oriented) resources ranging from

St. Augustine, Richard Rohr, Teilhard de Chardin; Adam Hamilton, "How Great Thou Art"; Thomas Keating, Lee Strobel, Barbara Brown Taylor; the Dalai Lama, Martin Luther King: "When I Survey the Wondrous Cross"; the Navajo Great Spirit; St. Francis of Assisi; "Amazing Grace"; John Newton; Joan Rivers; Paul (from the Bible); the Lone Ranger; Henri Nouwen; Helen Keller; Charles Schultz and Peanuts; Red Skelton…what a diverse, star-studded supporting cast… and all are interrelated and germane to both the chapter theme as well as to the overall development of this creative book.

This is not just a "head" book; I would describe this creative composition as one of the best heart, mind, body, and soul books I have ever read! Lots of pithy, deep, meaningful references! Many resources and exercises allow the reader to grow as much as humanly possible. "With God's help" would be a phrase to invoke as the reader travels through this uplifting and enlightening book. Terms are defined well, and ideas are probed and developed meaningfully. Chapter 6, titled, Bad Friday/ Good Friday, is a prime example where through the use of four very cleverly constructed questions, the reader is walked through everything you wanted to know about the crucifixion through the understandable various theories of atonement, and through Weatherhead's presentation on "the Will of God!" Again, great overview, but also attention to detail; well presented in only ten pages! After the development, and references to works by Richard Rohr discussed and analyzed, Jim Wagner lays this nugget (among many others) in your lap: "Jesus did not come to change the mind of God about humanity, but Jesus came to change the mind of humanity about God!" Whew…made me really stop and reflect! There is so much well-presented material in this book to assist you, whatever your position, for meaningful spiritual growth! To me this book is like a humongous tapestry…many, many threads, but all interwoven to provide an enriching tapestry of spiritual examination and growth experience!

Being a professor emeritus in education, I have written, read, helped compose, critiqued, analyzed...many education "productions" of the last 45 years. I can say without any reservation that this particular creative publication is one of the best ever. After reading and rereading the book, I still have no idea how the author collected and wove so many thoughts/ ideas/references/exercises/challenges/personal sharing and resources. I invite you, and possibly with friends, to carefully journey through this book. Thank you, Rev. Jim Wagner, from the bottom of my heart (and mind, body, and soul) for this work that you and God created! AND, just when you think you could not possibly learn any more...and you've gained so much by reading, reflecting, and growing spiritually...Jim Wagner comes along with his last chapter 15 (which is 50 percent longer than any other chapter). And this chapter is even more spiritually loaded than any of the other 14 chapters. The title is most appropriately named "But Wait, There's More"... and so much more! He not only "tells" but again "shares" much of himself and his spiritual experiences in the closing pages (i.e., his life-long developed personal credo). I know you will enjoy this wonderful book as you read and ponder its timely and timeless messages.

John Hinton
Professor Emeritus Otterbein University, Mathematics Education.
Spiritual Formation and Development Studies with Wellstream
(Spirituality Network),
Dallas Theological Seminary, and Ashland Theological Seminary.

INTRODUCTION

Living in a retirement community, as I do, offers an inside look at attitudes, behavior patterns, and personal values as expressed by older adults, whose ages range from 66 to 100, with the average being 85 years old. In the 21st century, age 65 is no longer the mandatory time to "hang it up," take it easy, and shift into an inactive mode. Today's 60-year-olds function more like former 50-year-olds; 70-year-olds are the new 60s; those in their 80s have as much vigor and vitality as previous 70-year-olds; 90-year-olds are reported to be the fastest growing segment of the American population; and whereas 100-year-olds used to be something of a rarity, in today's world centenarians are quite common. Gerontologists are busy rewriting and updating formerly assumed data. For instance here is one of the current projections of aging in three stages:

> 65 to 74 = Young Old
> 75 to 84 = Old Old
> 85 & over = Oldest Old

How does one account for these significant elder changes? Perhaps an apt analogy would be to compare automobiles made in the 1950s to those manufactured today. In mid-20th century, if you owned a car and the odometer turned 100,000 miles, that was the moment to begin thinking about trading for a newer model. Not so anymore. Many auto owners today would say that the first 100,000 miles have served as the "breaking in" period. If everything mechanical is working well, then aiming for the 200,000-mile mark is a reasonable goal.

Just as today's automobiles have been vastly improved following the latest technological and engineering research, so has the health of older adults benefitted from tremendous advances in medicine, especially as related to the aging process. We are bombarded via TV, magazines, newspapers, social media, doctors, therapists, family, and friends encouraging us to develop wholesome and active lifestyles (paying attention to calories, eating a healthy diet, physical fitness and exercise, social interaction, and mental alertness). Yet, granted these are all good, what about the spiritual dimensions of our lives? Are we paying attention to our soul and our relationship with our Creator?

David Hilton, M.D., former staff member of the Christian Medical Commission (World Council of Churches), is convinced that:

> "the most important dimension to health is the spiritual. Even in the midst of poverty some people stay well, while among the world's affluent many are chronically ill. Why? Medical science is beginning to affirm that one's beliefs and feelings are the ultimate tools and powers for healing. Unresolved guilt, anger, resentment, and meaninglessness are found to be the greatest suppressors of the body's powerful, health-controlling immune system, while loving relationships in community are among its strongest augmenters. Those in harmony with the Creator, and the earth, and their neighbors not only survive tragedy and suffering best, but grow stronger in the process."[1]

The title of this book came from an article I read in the *National Geographic* magazine: "The World's Oldest People." A man living in southern Russia claimed to be 130 and drank vodka every day for breakfast. Goat yogurt is attributed to long life among the people of Mongolia. But a comment by this citizen of Ecuador may cause you to smile. He lamented, "Being 123 has its limitations. Oh, to be 108 again."

Notice the subtitle: "Aging gracefully by living fully in the fourth quarter of life." When older adults reflect seriously on life's journey, they sometimes divide their years into four seasons: spring, summer, autumn, and winter. Some view their life's experiences similar to a play in three acts. Personally, I think about my life as moving in and through four observable quarters: first quarter ages 1-25; second quarter 25-50; third quarter 50-75; fourth quarter 75 and older. These are not necessarily precise and not intended for "one size fits all." There could well be some overlap. As I am now living into my fourth quarter I encourage you, at whatever stage you view yourself, to be as intentional as possible in taking seriously your spiritual self. I fully agree with Richard L. Morgan, who coined the phrase "No wrinkles on the soul."[2]

Although my body is captive to the aging process and my memory is not what it used to be, my spiritual self has never been more alive and sensitive to life's abundant wonders, great and small. Living in the fourth quarter may mean retirement from our working years, but it can increase growth, appreciation, and enjoyment of our spiritual life.

Ongoing studies and conversations related to maximum life span always get our attention. Gerontologists are now predicting (based on medical research and healthy lifestyles) that babies born after the year 2,000 could well live to be 120. Five-generation families will become the norm. However, the bottom line is this: Because the human race has a 100 percent mortality rate, the question is not how many years do I have left but rather, how am I living out all the years I do have? While wrinkles on the skin tend to multiply, I do believe my soul is wrinkle-free; therefore, I am asking myself and encouraging you to ask yourself: what are some ways I can be more intentional, more aware, and more responsive to the spiritual dimensions of life? Ponder this affirmation by the famed Swiss psychiatrist Dr. Carl Jung (1875–1961) who noted that none of his patients in the second half of their lives (after age 35) recovered unless they developed a religious attitude, not necessarily a commitment to a specific tradition or creed, but rather a personal spirituality, an individual connection to sacred reality.[3]

The science of aging is coming up with some intriguing concepts. One study suggests that human beings actually have four different ages all at once.

1. Chronological Age: This is determined by the number of years we have lived since the year we were born. What year were you born? What year is this? That's your chronological age.
2. Biological Age: The condition of your physical health determines your biological age. When my 90-year-old mother had her eyes examined, the ophthalmologist told her that she had the eyes and eyesight of a 50-year-old.
3. Psychological Age: How you feel and how you act is your psychological age. Ever have someone tell you to act your age?
4. Spiritual Age: Although more difficult to measure, ask yourself if you feel you are still in the kindergarten of spirituality or are you moving on to spiritual maturity?
5. The Apostle Paul alerts us to our ongoing spiritual development: "So we do not lose heart. Even though our outer nature is wasting away (the aging process) our inner nature is being renewed day by day" (2 Corinthians 4:16 RSV).

I understand my inner nature as my spiritual heart and soul. When President John Quincy Adams was 80 years old a friend asked him, "And how are you, John?" With a twinkle in his eye he replied, "John Quincy Adams is well, thank you, but the house in which he lives is sadly dilapidated. I think John Quincy Adams will have to move out before long."

With older adults in mind I have written this book, not as a self-proclaimed expert, or as a professional gerontologist, but as one who has come to appreciate and care deeply about the uniqueness of aging and the joy of awakening each day thankful for the gift of life. What I have learned and am still learning I share with each reader. A word about this book's format. The chapters begins with questions that I have been asked or heard discussed by older adults. Reflections on these questions are rooted in the soil of life's uncertainties and the day-by-day perseverance of undaunted, aging, wise human beings. In some tribal societies the elders are called "The Wisdom Bearers" and are accorded the highest respect, as noted in the Old Testament: "In old age is wisdom; understanding in a long life" (Book of Job 12:12 CEB).

Consider this remarkable story in the Book of Genesis, chapters 37-50. The spotlight is on Joseph, who was sold into slavery by his jealous brothers and landed in Egypt. Many years later came a devastating famine throughout the Middle Eastern world, except in Egypt, where there was a surplus of food. As the story goes the great Hebrew patriarch Jacob, along with his many sons and their families, made the long trip from Palestine to Egypt to buy food. Upon arrival, Jacob discovered, much to his total amazement, that his son Joseph was not only alive but also the governor of Egypt in charge of food distribution, and a personal friend of the pharaoh. Following a tender and tearful reunion, Joseph took his father to meet the pharaoh. The pharaoh did not say, "Welcome, Jacob," or "So pleased to meet you."

In customary Middle Eastern fashion, the pharaoh's first words were "How old are you?" Although that may seem like a strange way to greet someone, not so in that country and culture. The older a person was, the more revered and honored was that person.

> Joseph says, "O Great Pharaoh, I want you to meet my father Jacob."
> The Pharaoh says, "How old are you?"
> Jacob responds, "I am 130 years old." (Genesis 47:7-10 CEB)

And the two of them are off to a beautiful relationship.

In my associations, interactions, and conversations, I have been blessed by many contemporary "Wisdom Bearers," some of whom you will meet in this book. As you begin to read and turn the pages you might make a list of those gracious elders in your life who freely shared their wisdom and whose stories have influenced and continue to shape your values, attitudes, and actions.

"A Spiritual and Ethical Wellness Checklist" is included for your personal use. (See Appendix A.) This brief exercise can help you identify those areas and issues that could be nourished and cultivated. There are no right or wrong answers. I call it "priming the pump" (something like pouring a small amount of water down a hand pump to get the water flowing from a deep well). Be as honest as you can in responding to the 25 statements. At the end of each chapter are questions to ponder. These are designed for personal reflection. It may be helpful to keep a note pad close by to record your thoughts and insights. Small groups could use these questions and your personal notes as springboards for sharing and discussion sessions. (See Appendix B.) As you read and reflect on various topics related to aging in each chapter, consider this question: What are some ways I could be more intentional in developing my spirituality and living gracefully in my fourth quarter of life?

Chapter 1

SOUL AND SPIRITUALITY

*"Something of God flows into us from the blue
of the sky, the taste of honey, the delicious
embrace of water and even sleep itself."*
—C. S. Lewis

Question: "Soul is a very common word in our everyday lives and language, but I have never had a discussion with anyone about 'soul' nor have I ever heard a sermon on 'soul.' So, what do we mean when we use this word?"

Reflection: As I pondered this question put to me by my 94-year-old friend, I had to agree with her. A quick answer was not appropriate and caused me to search my own interpretation of this word so prevalent, yet so elusive. To understand what I mean or intend to imply when I use the word "soul," I also needed to explore a related concept: "spirituality."

We glibly talk about soul food…soul music…soul sister or soul brother…the soul of our city or country. Amazingly I discovered that the word "soul" is recorded over 500 times in the Bible. Interestingly, in the Hebrew Scriptures (Old Testament) and in the Greek Scriptures (New Testament), the word for "soul" can be translated several ways in the English language: breath, life, vitality, desire, mind, spirit, heart, being, soul.

To illustrate: Psalm 103:1 in the King James Version (KJV), "Bless the Lord, O my soul and all that is within me, bless his holy name." The same verse in the Common English Bible (CEB), "Let my whole being bless the Lord! Let everything inside me bless his holy name!"

The Greeks taught that human beings have souls within their physical bodies, believing that when the body dies the soul continues to exist. Whereas the body is temporary, the immortal soul goes on forever. One tradition in Judaism claims that the body and soul are intertwined. They may be separated for a while when the body dies, but will be reunited in the next life. All of the major religions of the world have their own interpretation of "soul." A common or universally accepted definition is nonexistent. Likewise, even within Christianity opinions and beliefs are not consistent.

My personal understanding of "soul" begins with the Creation story: "God created humanity in God's own image. God created them male and female" (Genesis 1:27). Because God is spiritual and not physical, I believe that I am a spiritual being created in God's image and, for a few years, have human experiences in and through my physical body. Furthermore, when my body can no longer function, my divine nature/spirit/soul continues to exist. My soul is the essence of who I am, my personality, the very core of my being. My soul is that which makes me unique as a creation of God.

To recap, consider this interpretation of soul:

- the true self
- the self unmasked
- the unique inner self, hidden, yet always present
- the dynamic, powerful, positive influence within our being that enables us to experience grace, mercy, love, and forgiveness

Next consider these related words: spirituality, spiritual, spirit. As with the concept of soul these are common words in our everyday speech, but without a commonly accepted definition or description. Spirituality is a broad term with room for many perspectives. Generally speaking, it includes a sense of connection to something greater than ourselves, and it typically involves a search for meaning in life. "Spiritual" has a variety of usages pertaining to one's spirit or soul as distinguished from one's physical nature. Perhaps you have heard someone say, "Well, I am spiritual, but not religious."

Things really get complicated when trying to define spirit and spirituality. My unabridged dictionary records 31 definitions and 29 synonyms for spirit. A helpful understanding of spirituality is this interpretation by John Mogabgab, the founding editor of *Weavings* magazine published by The Upper Room Ministries in Nashville, TN:

"The spiritual life does not begin with special knowledge and end in flight from the world. Simplicity locates the spiritual life where it belongs—in the ordinary events of life. The spiritual life leads to the very heart of the world... Daily life careens across the surface of a vast reality whose ancient depths hold unseen beauty and truth. We live and move and have our very being only because of this reality and yet remain largely unaware of its presence."[4]

Spirituality is more about being than doing, more about awareness than action, more about mindfulness than busyness, more about seeing than performing. Spirituality encompasses the human search for something more than the possession and constant accumulation of "stuff." Spirituality deals with the dynamics of the heart. Sixteen hundred years ago Augustine, in his timeless and often quoted prayer, underscored this spiritual hunger: "Our hearts are restless, O God, until they rest in you."

Another expression of this same thought comes from Joyce Venaglia (a former nun). "God's life within us is God's most precious gift to us. How we respond to this incredible gift through our thoughts, words, and actions creates our own individual spirituality."

I am convinced that deep within our DNA is a desire to communicate with our Creator, who also yearns to communicate with us. This universal two-way dialogue is called prayer, a significant and primary experience that we will explore in a later chapter. Pause a moment to reflect on this statement attributed to French philosopher/theologian Pierre Teilhard de Chardin (1881–1955).

"We are not human beings having a spiritual experience.
We are spiritual beings having a human experience."

As we proceed I invite you to think about your personal word for the Creator of the cosmos, the universe, the galaxies, the stars, and all that is included in the creation of Planet Earth. Notice that I have been referring to the Creator as God, a common word, yet not universally used or accepted by all human beings. In the literature of Alcoholics Anonymous the word "God" is not printed. Instead it refers to a "greater power." Native American prayer is often addressed to the "Great Spirit." There are more than 100 names for God in the Bible. The Muslim tradition provides a practice for meditating on 99 names for Allah (the one God). The faithful in the Hindu religion worship one great God, who is manifested in countless numbers of deities.

Buddhism, on the other hand, has no mention of God and appears to be more of a philosophy or way of life. Our human vocabulary is totally inadequate to define or describe what Karl Rahner calls "the incomprehensible Holy Mystery." Or as Adrian van Kaam puts it: "Life is a mystery to be lived, not a problem to be solved." So I repeat the question: What is your personal word or phrase for the Creator of all creation? Think about that, then write it down for further pondering.

This brings us to spiritual formation, a two-word phrase intended to highlight not only the importance of recognizing our inherent spiritual nature, but also to encourage intentionality in shaping and forming one's spirituality, sometimes called "spiritual growth." Question: whose spirit or what spirituality is your spiritual nature following these days? Is it Christian, Muslim, Jewish, Hindu, Buddhist, secular humanist, agnostic, or what? Those who claim no affiliation with organized religion are sometimes labeled "nones." However, "nones" still seek to satisfy their inherent spirituality by pursuing their personal values and loyalties, such as family, education, career, health, wealth, possessions, country, celebrities, politics, or (fill in the blank). Untold numbers of persons, although they have no formal religious ties, claim certain moral and ethical standards: you are a good person if you don't harm or bother anyone, if you don't commit a major crime, if you pay your taxes, if you are tolerant and accepting of a variety of lifestyles. Though these are worthwhile goals, do they satisfy and fulfill one's need for something more as reflected in a once popular song titled: "Is That All There Is?"

Our spirituality is shaped and formed by our primary loyalties and personal values. Here is how Richard Rohr states this universal truth: "So everybody has a god, or one central reference point, whether they admit it or not. All you need is a god who is really worthy of being God. Because you will become (like) the god you worship."[5]

Take some moments to reflect on these descriptions of spiritual formation.

"The process or practice by which a person may progress in one's spiritual or religious life." —Wikipedia Internet

"Thirst for God is a lodestone of holy yearning that draws us into the caverns of the heart and the byways of the world seeking the only One who can relieve our privation (lack of what is needed)." —John Mogabgab

"The process whereby we grow in relationship with God and become conformed to Christ." —Upper Room Ministries

This personal story by Rev. Bruce Ough (United Methodist Church Bishop) spotlights the essence of spiritual formation.

"Years ago when I was just beginning my pastoral ministry, I made my first week long spiritual retreat at Harmony Hills, a Roman Catholic Benedictine convent and retreat center in Watertown, South Dakota. When I arrived at the center, I discovered one of the sisters had been assigned to be my host. I have forgotten her name, but I remember she had a great sense of humor and was most gracious. She would check with me several times each day to make sure I was comfortable and that my retreat was going well. On the third day she invited me to participate in community prayer times. I thought, *Why not?* It would be a great learning experience, and perhaps enrich my personal prayer time. I soon learned that Benedictine communities pray at least four times a day—very early in the morning, before lunch, late afternoon, and evening. Two days into this regimen, I remember the sister asking me how my retreat was going and if the community prayers were helpful. My immediate reply was 'I am enjoying the prayer times, but I find them somewhat disruptive to my schedule. I

6

have been wondering how you sisters get anything done around here. You just get started doing something and the bell is ringing, calling you to prayer again.' The sister paused. I could see her humor begin to dance in her eyes. I knew I was caught! Then she spoke. 'That is the problem with you Protestants. You think doing God's work is staying busy. We believe doing God's work is being attentive to God'."6

Being attentive to God every day in various ways with intentional spiritual practices is the engine that drives and develops our spirituality. Having been baptized and confirmed in the Roman Catholic Church and later ordained in The United Methodist Church, I wrote this book through the lens of Christian spirituality and my personal experiences as a minister/pastor. Although my lifelong commitment to Jesus Christ is reflected throughout these pages, my purpose is to be an encourager with readers of all faith traditions, as well as those with no religious ties, in developing one's own unique spirituality. The topics in this book speak to our common experiences as we cope with the aging process, such as solitude, loneliness, grief, health, prayer, eternal life, faith, love, forgiveness, compassion, gratitude, humor, and grace.

QUESTIONS TO PONDER

1. What are some spiritual issues or questions you are dealing with at this time in your life?

2. "We are not human beings having a spiritual experience. We are spiritual beings having a human experience." How do you respond to Teilhard's statement?

3. What is your personal understanding of soul, spirit, spirituality, spiritual formation?

4. Name your personal goals for spiritual growth and formation.

Chapter 2

SOLITUDE AND SILENCE

"Inner silence is absence of any sort of
inward stirring of thought or emotion, but it is
complete alertness, openness to God."
—Anthony Bloom

Question: "I'm having difficulty understanding 'Be still and know that I am God' (Psalm 46:10 NRSV). Life is so fast-paced and noisy that silence is hard to find. How can you 'be still' in today's kind of world?"

Reflection: This question may seem a bit odd to be raised by an older adult. Yet people of all ages seem to be immersed in sound throughout their waking hours. When visiting "retirees" (whether in their homes or in retirement communities) I find the TV is usually on, not being paid much attention, but providing background sounds. Does this serve to dispel some of their loneliness? Is this the result of not being taught to appreciate solitude and silence? Yet, nurturing one's spirituality begins with an intentionality about solitude and silence. This seems to be easier for introverted persons, whereas those who are heavier on the extroverted scale might have more difficulty. However, whatever your personality type, engaging regularly in solitude and silence is a worthwhile and doable goal.

It is important to distinguish between being alone and experiencing loneliness. To be physically separated from other human beings is to be alone. Whereas, loneliness is an emotional separation from others, a feeling of being disconnected, overlooked, or ignored. Loneliness is one of the most universal human experiences impacting all ages at all stages in life. One can have deep feelings of loneliness in the midst of a crowd. Think of what it was like on your first day at a new job, or enrolling in a new school, or attending a party and when you arrived you knew no one and no one paid attention to you. In those situations you were not alone but you were experiencing loneliness.

Many who are living in their fourth quarter of life live alone. Some may have multiple opportunities for social interaction, while others may not. In either situation emotional feelings of loneliness lurk nearby. In his insightful book *Beyond Loneliness: The Gift of God's Friendship*, Trevor Howard addresses this reality of aging.

"Hidden within our loneliness lies a treasure, the longing that God placed in our hearts for divine friendship... Deep within us there is hole that only God's living presence can fill."[7]

Many fourth-quarter elders have an abundance of solitude, unlike those earlier years when it was a challenge just to carve out some alone time away from the company of others. A young mother once confided that in order to enjoy quiet time away from her children, she went to the bathroom and locked the door for a few minutes of privacy, meditation, and prayer. One of my pastor friends developed the habit of driving to his nearest McDonald's restaurant very early on Sunday mornings, locating a quiet booth and working silently on his soon-to-be-delivered sermon while drinking coffee away from family

sounds and interruptions. So, whether you do or do not live in solitude, seriously consider designating a portion of each day to focus
100 percent on nurturing your spiritual friendship with God.

Doing this on a regular basis is highlighted by the noted author and
spiritual director Henri J. M. Nouwen.

"Without solitude it is virtually impossible to live a spiritual life.
Solitude begins with a time and place for God and God alone."[8]

The Message Bible offers a contemporary translation of Matthew 6:6,
where Jesus instructed his disciples: "Here is what I want you to do.
Find a quiet, secluded place so you won't be tempted to role play
before God. Just be there simply and as honestly as you can manage. The focus will shift from you to God and you will begin to sense
God's grace."

An anonymous monk moves this thought to the next level: "Spiritual
solitude is not simply being alone, but keeping connected to God
while one is alone."[9]

So, begin by eliminating distracting sounds to achieve 100 percent
quietness.

However, observing silence, practicing silence, appreciating silence,
teaching silence are not to be found in our churches, schools, and
community organizations. "Some studies show that the average group
can tolerate only about fifteen seconds of silence before someone
feels compelled to break it, and our Sunday (church) services give
little reason to doubt this finding," writes Parker J. Palmer.[10]

The benefits and blessings of cultivating solitude and silence are only
experienced by those who initiate and practice this spiritual discipline.

Practitioner Susan Muto shares her positive witness: "Silence is not to be shunned as empty space but to be befriended as fertile ground for intimacy with God. Spiritual masters, both Western and Eastern, point out that silence is a condition for being and remaining present to the Transcendent (God). Experience also confirms that silence fosters relaxation and may increase efficiency."[11]

Think for a minute what you would need to do to set the stage for a time of intentional solitude and silence. Step one is turning off all electronic communication devices, including the TV. Some say that playing soft music in the background provides a meditative environment. While that may be relaxing, is it conducive to sensing God's presence and listening for that still, small voice? Personally, I need to turn off the music for total quietness. Recall this highly unusual

experience of the Prophet Elijah, who in an attempt to hide from his enemies sought refuge in a cave. The Lord then instructed Elijah to go outside and stand on the mountain so that he could know the Lord's presence was with him. Then there arose a mighty wind so strong it split mountains and broke rocks in pieces, but the Lord was not in the wind; after the wind came an earthquake, but the Lord was not in the earthquake; after that came a fire, but the Lord was not in the fire; and after the fire came a still, small voice (the sound of sheer silence). Only then was Elijah totally receptive to the divine presence and to receiving messages from the Lord (I Kings 19:11-13 CEB).

In cultivating divine friendship by practicing solitude and silence, be mindful that the pattern is the same way we develop person-to-person friendship:

- spending time together
- learning about each other
- being honest and transparent

- listening to each other
- allowing for changing views of each other
- enjoying just being together silently[12]

After creating your personal space and surrounding yourself with silence, begin with a brief centering prayer, something like a prelude or the first step toward being fully present to the Holy Presence. Here are some centering prayers I find helpful:

Now I close the door of my spirit to all except the Spirit of Christ as I wait and listen with the ears of my soul. Amen.

Holy Spirit, help me to be aware of your Presence, promptings, and nudges, as we spend this time together. Amen.

Gracious and Loving God, forgive me when I allow less important matters to distract me from spending more time with you. During these special moments I want to focus 100 percent on you and to be receptive to any thought or word you may have for me today. Thank you. Amen.

I find it helpful to repeat a brief prayer several times to focus my thoughts, get comfortable with the silence, and open my spiritual receptors to listen and to receive. You, of course, are encouraged to write your own centering prayers and to discover your own way of entering silence and solitude. Many excellent guides have been published to instruct us and encourage us in this spiritual practice. In the Bibliography I list several books and sources dealing with centering prayer, meditation, and contemplation. Another suggestion is to have a pen and notebook nearby to record anything that comes to you during the sacred silence. Some days you may be prompted to write much or little. And some days nothing will get your attention. That's okay. Simply be grateful for your specially designated time together in undisturbed communion and communication.

Here are some entry points that can assist in being more present to God's presence during intentional times of solitude and silence:

Hymns: Martin Luther, the 16th century Reformer, commented that after the Bible, his hymn book was the greatest source for spiritual insights and meditation. Simply reading and reflecting on the lyrics can be highly inspiring.

Praying the Psalms: The Book of Psalms has been tagged "The Prayer Book of the Bible." A minister shared with me that during his quiet time with God, he practices reading a Psalm until a word or a sentence causes him to pause. Rarely does he get through a complete Psalm before experiencing a nudge to stop, reflect, meditate, and pray.

For a more structured spiritual exercise, see the format by Beth Richardson in Appendix C.

Reflect on this helpful and encouraging word by Ruth Haley Barton:

"The invitation to solitude and silence is just that. It is an invitation to enter more deeply into the intimacy of a relationship with the One who waits just outside the noise and busyness of our lives. It is an invitation to communication and communion with the One who is always present even when our awareness has been dulled by distraction. It is an invitation to the adventure of spiritual transformation in the deepest places of our being, an adventure that will result in greater freedom and authenticity and surrender to God."[13]

Practicing the spiritual discipline of solitude and silence every day does yield amazing results. Here are some of the blessings I have experienced:

- bonds my connection with God.
- helps me manage stress better.
- gives my mind, body, and spirit "time out" for relaxation and recreation.
- puts my priorities in order.
- centers and strengthens the foundations of my faith.
- invites and allows the Holy Spirit to move, act, and guide in my life as I pray about anything and everything.
- motivates me to pray more regularly for family, friends, strangers, situations.
- gives the Healing Christ opportunities to touch and heal at all levels of my being and in all areas of my life.
- makes me more mindful of the peace of God that surpasses all human understanding (Philippians 4:7 CEB).[14]

QUESTIONS TO PONDER

1. What have been some of your experiences with solitude and silence?

2. Is anything preventing you from being more intentional in having time alone with God? If so, name some of those distractions, obstacles, or personal challenges.

3. Whether you live alone or in a family and group setting, could you designate some time and space each day for intentional silence, centering prayer, and receptive listening?

4. On a scale of one to ten, with ten being the highest mark, how do you evaluate your relationship with God? Keep in mind that this can fluctuate from day to day and that in God's eyes you are always "a ten."

Chapter 3

PRAYER: INTERNET OF THE SOUL

*"Do not worry about anything, but in everything by
prayer and supplication (petition) with thanksgiving,
let your requests be made known to God."*
(Philippians 4:6 NRSV).

Questions: "The older I get, it seems the more I pray. Yet, I find myself asking what is prayer? Can prayer really make a difference? Are some kinds of prayers more helpful than others? Does God always answer prayer?"

Reflection: Think of spending time with your very best friend. Sometimes you listen, sometimes you talk, sometimes you simply enjoy being together without speaking words. This is exactly the way prayer works. There seems to be something embedded in humanity's DNA that prompts us to communicate with our Creator. James Miller explains this credible theory in his book *Hardwired: Finding the God You Already Know.*[15] Taking our cue from the Book of Genesis 1:27, human beings are created in the image of God (who is spiritual not physical). Anthropologists are discovering that tribes, cultures, societies, and ethnic people throughout this planet have devised various ways of channeling their adoration, petitions, and prayers to the One who is nameless, yet goes by many names.

In the Jewish-Christian tradition we are taught that prayer is like a conduit that directly connects the created ones with the Creator. The Bible conveys story after story of our Creator's desire to be in a loving relationship with all of humanity. Perhaps that is why the words "pray" and "prayer" are recorded over 500 times in the Bible with similar meanings in both the Hebrew (OT) and Greek (NT) scriptures: "to worship, to adore, to ask, to petition." In a sense prayer is similar to an ongoing conversation, as stated so well by Robert Farrar Capon: "Prayer is just talking to someone who is already talking to you… listening to someone who is already listening to you."[16]

Right now, complete this sentence: For me prayer is _____. Then jot down any questions or issues related to prayer that you might have. Next, compare your thoughts to the following definitions, descriptions, and high regards for prayer.

The more you pray, the more you want to pray. The less you pray, the more you know something is missing in your life. —Anonymous

Prayer is not a substitute for action. Prayer is an action for which there is no substitute. —Anonymous

Pray all the time. If necessary use words. —Anonymous

Prayer is being polite enough to listen to God. —Anonymous

Prayer is giving God loving attention. —St. Teresa of Avila

Pray always and do not lose heart. —Jesus (Luke 18:1)

18

To be a Christian without praying is no more possible than to be alive without breathing. —Martin Luther King, Jr.

Prayer can be as simple as basking in the sunshine of God's love. —Alice Pinto

The real purpose of prayer is intimacy with God, not acquisition from God. —Steve Harper

Prayer is the soul's sincere desire, uttered or unexpressed. —James Montgomery

Prayer is like using the telephone. Sometimes you talk, sometimes you listen. —Six-year-old girl

I always come away from my prayer times with the feeling that just when I am ready to stop, God is ready to begin. —Douglas Steer

The seventeenth-century Archbishop Fenlon gave us a powerful metaphor for prayer: "The wind of God is always blowing, but you have to hoist your sail." Think of prayer as hoisting your spiritual sail in order to go with the flow of God's Spirit day after day after day.

Perhaps you have seen the painting that depicts an artist's concept of Christ standing outside a house. "Listen! I am standing at the door knocking. If you hear my voice and open the door, I will come in to be with you and you with me" (Revelation 3:20 CEB).

One interpretation is that the door represents the human heart or soul. The most striking feature of that painting is the absence of a handle on the door. It can only be opened from the inside. This implies that no matter how long or how loud is the knocking, the person inside has the option to open or not open the door to the One, who patiently waits to come in, but never huffs and puffs and blows the door down.

To put that another way, God gave you and all humanity a very precious gift called "free will." This means that God respects our human freedom and individual choices. When you and I pray we are essentially giving God permission to move, to act, to influence, to guide, to direct, to bring resources into our lives. Think of prayer as cooperation with God; think of prayer as putting God first in our lives and situations; think of prayer as allowing God to have the driver's seat and be in control. Do not think of prayer as you would a spare tire to pull out and put on only when you have an emergency.

I read that most all prayers can be "boiled down" to two types: "thank you" prayers and "help me" prayers. Think about that for a moment. Do your personal prayers fall into these two categories? I find myself frequently offering prayers of thanksgiving; likewise, I often engage in petitioning God to help me, my family, friends, strangers, victims of natural disasters, and people in war-ravaged countries. "Help me" prayers and "thank you" prayers are certainly honored by our compassionate and generous God. However, let's widen and enlarge our prayer scope.

We begin with the familiar saying: "Prayer changes things." Yes, I affirm that people and situations can be influenced by prayer; however, my personal experience is that prayer also changes the one doing the praying. For example, I have had some people in my life who did not treat me fairly or who intentionally disrespected me. Rather than nurse my hurt feelings and

build up tons of resentment, I have learned to pray by name for those who are insensitive and rude by asking God to bless them, their families, and their personal situations in life. Result: by sincerely praying that way for several days, weeks, or months, my attitude becomes more positive toward that person and my feelings of resentment melt away.

Some people feel their prayer life is inadequate because they do not know the correct words. The desire to communicate with God begins not with words, but in one's heart and soul. This comforting teaching by the Apostle Paul speaks to all of us when words fail in our prayer life: "The Spirit helps us in our weakness, for we do not know how to pray as we ought, but that very Spirit intercedes for us with sighs too deep for words" (Romans 8:28 CEB).

The Eastern Orthodox Churches teach three ways of praying:

1. Prayer of the lips (words spoken or written)
2. Prayer of the mind (meditation)
3. Prayer of the heart (contemplation)

Prayer of the lips is perhaps the most common. Think of praying "The Lord's Prayer" silently or aloud in worship services. Printed prayer and devotional books are available and helpful. We have much to learn from those in our faith tradition who came before we were born, as well as contemporary spiritual teachers. We are blessed with their wisdom and role models. Meditating or focusing our mind on a verse of scripture or basking in the glow of a sunrise/sunset or extended gazing on artwork or anything of beauty—this, too, can be prayer.

Of these three ways of praying, I find that contemplative prayer or prayer of the heart is the one least familiar. Basically this is listening and waiting, coming into God's presence without a personal agenda, being tuned to God's frequency prepared for what might come up. In Chapter 2, "Solitude and Silence," I emphasized repeating brief sentence prayers as an avenue into an unhurried time of intentional silence and listening. Along with that suggestion consider what are called "Breath Prayers."

A breath prayer consists of two parts: your personal name for God and a brief phrase naming your personal desire of the moment. Some examples:

- Fill me with your fullness, Lord.
- Be still and know that I am God.
- With the ears of my soul, I listen, O God.
- Calming Spirit, quiet my mind and heart.
- My presence seeks your Presence.
- Listen, my soul, to hear the Lord.
- God, I need your peace.
- Peace of God be with me now.
- Lord Jesus, I wait and listen.
- Healing Christ, I need your health.

When praying your breath prayer, try to regulate your breathing so that you inhale on the first half of the prayer and exhale on the other half. Repeat this several times, either out loud or silently, until you are still and ready to listen. Do not rush. Conclude your contemplative prayer with thanksgiving and gratitude for this special time of solitude, silence, and being alone with God.

When I left home after graduating from high school and went off to college in Ohio, my family moved to Florida. I still treasure my mother's letters reminding me that she was praying for me every day. During my three years in military service, she was praying for me every day. Then in my seminary training and throughout my ministerial career, she was praying for me every day. I know her prayers blessed me beyond measure. We call that Intercessory Prayer (praying for others). No doubt my mother learned the value of praying this way from her mother, my grandmother, who lived to be 103 years old. The last few years of her life she was confined to her bed. One day when I visited her I asked, "Grandma, tell me what you think about, what do you do all day?" Her eyesight was gone so she no longer watched TV. Her answer, "First thing I do when I wake up each day is pray by name for everyone in our big family, scattered all over God's earth. Then after breakfast, I put on my headphones and listen to the radio. Even though I don't know the people who are in trouble or having a hard time, I pray for them. I know God will help and bless them."

Intercessory Prayer is honored by God, who blesses those being prayed for as well as blessing those who are praying. Also, when I intentionally pray for another person, I like to let them know about my caring and concern. Responses will vary from "Oh…really?" to "Thank you so much. Please keep praying." People need to know that others care for them. Another suggestion is to keep a notebook to list those for whom you are praying and the date. Then in three or four months look back over your entries and reflect on what has happened in the lives of those for whom you have prayed. Also, you might consider praying for everyone who sends you a Christmas card. I like to do this immediately upon opening each envelope. I save all of the cards until a month or so later. Then when I have an unhurried time I read each Christmas card and pray for the senders. Following this I cut up the cards and send the card-fronts to St. Jude's Ranch for Children in Nevada, where the cards are recycled and remade into new Christmas cards.[17]

Another excellent way of praying is keeping a gratitude journal. This is easy to do and brings a healthy perspective to your life. By your bedside have a notebook and pen. Before going to sleep write down at least five good things that happened to you during the past several hours (person, event, situation, or whatever). Research shows that thankful people tend to be healthier people.

Do you know about the increase/decrease prayer? I have found this way of praying to be quite effective when faced with choices in complicated situations, such as career moves, choosing a school, moving to another part of the country, medical procedures, financial decisions, and relationships. God desires and yearns to give us guidance in our lives:

> "I will instruct you and teach you in the direction you should go. I'll advise you and keep my eye on you" (Psalm 32:8 CEB).

Here is a sample format for increase/decrease prayers:

> Loving and Gracious God, I know you want only the best for me. Help me in making this decision to _____. If your will is for me to do this, increase my desire. If not, decrease my desire. With a grateful heart, I sincerely thank you. Amen!

Pray your increase/decrease prayer for several days or weeks until you have clarity on your decision. Then take action accordingly.

The world's libraries house multiple books on the art and significance of prayer; however, let it be said clearly that there are no rules or correct ways to pray, provided one's motivation is to engage in sincere dialogue with God. As the hymn goes: "What a privilege to carry everything to God in prayer."[18]

To the question "Does God always answer prayer?" one person glibly responded that God answers prayer in a variety of ways: Yes; No; Wait awhile; I thought you would never ask; You have got to be kidding. Even though my prayer results have not always been what I expected, I am convinced that God knows what is best for us and that the other half of the scripture I quoted at the beginning of this chapter is the dependable answer when we are faithful in our prayers.

"And the peace of God, which surpasses all understanding, will guard your hearts and your minds in Christ Jesus" (Philippians 4:7 NRSV).

Knowing, experiencing, being aware of "the peace of God" enables us to cope with all of life. This was the reason Brother Lawrence, the often quoted monk, could practice the presence of God while washing pots and pans in the kitchen. This is why it is said about Francis of Assisi that he not merely prayed, but that he became a prayer. Incorporating prayer in our lifestyle means becoming more aware and increasingly mindful of God's blessed presence anytime and anywhere.

In reflecting on my personal prayer life, I find myself increasingly in agreement with E. Stanley Jones, who wisely wrote:

"Prayer tones up the total life. I find by actual experience I am better or worse as I pray more or less. If my prayer life sags, my whole life sags with it; if my prayer life goes up, my life as a whole goes up with it. Prayer is not an optional subject in the curriculum of living. It is a required subject. And there is no graduation into adequate human living without prayer."[19]

Now consider this riddle: WHO AM I?

I am the God-given craving bred into every human heart.
I am the newborn's first breath and the dying one's last gasp.
I am the soul's sincere desire, uttered or unexpressed.
I am simple enough for small children to understand, yet profound enough to confound the wisest of the wise.
I am not learned in a classroom, but I am taught through all of life's experiences.
I am the subject of untold numbers of books, yet as fresh, as radiant, as inviting as the morning sun.

I am the communication link with the Holy One called God.
I am the primary spiritual therapy.
I am compassion felt and love expressed.
I am gratitude and thanksgiving.
I am petition.
I am meditation.
I am contemplation.
I can be very wordy or I can be totally silent.
I am at home with those in solitude, as well as those in a multitude.
I am the Internet of the soul, reaching outward around the world and reaching inward to all in my personal world.

WHO AM I?   I AM PRAYER!

****

QUESTIONS TO PONDER

1. Earlier in this chapter you were invited to write out your personal definition or description of prayer. Do you want to keep your prayer statement as is or are you prompted to do some editing?

2. Taking our cue from the Nike slogan "Just do it," what are some obstacles or impediments that seem to prevent you from developing prayer as your lifestyle?

3. Of these various ways to pray, which ones might you want to practice in your prayer life?

   Intercessory Prayer; Centering Prayer; Breath Prayer; Increase/Decrease Prayer;

   Keeping a Gratitude Journal; Petition; Meditation; Contemplation

4. Does this thought by Richard Rohr fit your understanding of prayer or cause you to rethink the heart and nature of prayer?

   "The word prayer has often been trivialized by making it a way of getting what we want. But I use prayer as the umbrella word for any interior journey or practices that allow us to experience faith, hope, and love within ourselves. It is not a technique for getting things, a pious exercise that somehow makes God happy, or a requirement for entry into heaven. It is much more like practicing heaven now."[20]

Chapter 4

THE BIBLE: WIDELY PURCHASED/ NOT WIDELY READ

"If you want true knowledge of the scriptures, try to secure steadfast humility of heart, to carry you by the perfection of love not to knowledge that puffs up, but that enlightens."
—John Cassian (c.365–c.435)

Question: After putting it off for several years, I finally read the Bible from cover to cover. I found some parts very inspiring, other verses quite confusing and non-inspiring. Why is the Bible so difficult to understand?

Reflection: The word "bible" comes from the Latin word "biblia," which means "books." When you pick up a Bible you are actually holding a library of books, with a total of 66 divided into two main parts: the Old Testament or Hebrew Scriptures with 39 and the New Testament or Greek Scriptures with 27. Several factors contribute to the difficulty in understanding the Bible. Written over 1,000-plus years, by many authors, addressing readers from different cultures and countries, and not arranged in chronological order, the Bible presents a variety of challenges to comprehending its pages. The first five books in the Old Testament are known as the Torah or Law. These are followed by 12 books on the history of Israel, then five called poetry and wisdom books. Seventeen books referring to the Prophets complete the Old Testament. Likewise, the New Testament contains specific types of books categorized as the four Gospels, the Book of Acts, 21 Epistles or Letters to churches, and the Book of Revelation. Unless you can read and understand the Hebrew and Greek languages, you must rely on translations of the scriptures. For the English-speaking world there are over 50 Bible translations. The American Bible Society produces the Bible in dozens of the world's languages, making them available at a modest cost.[21]

When questions are raised about some of the inconsistencies of the Bible, keep in mind that very few original manuscripts still exist and that most of the contents were handed on from generation to generation by word of mouth, called the oral tradition or storytelling. For instance, this is why in the Book of Genesis we have two stories of Creation and why the Gospels of Matthew and Luke have different versions of the birth of Jesus, and although all four Gospel writers affirm the Resurrection of Jesus, they are inconsistent in reporting the details. The original biblical manuscripts did not delineate chapters and verses. In the year 1250, chapter numbers were added; verses were first marked in 1551. Before the invention of the printing press in the 16th century, the Bible was handwritten, page by page, a labor-intensive process that accounts for some of the textual differences.

Nevertheless, today's Bible readers have a variety of resources to assist with interpretation and understanding, such as Concordances, which translate the Hebrew and Greek words as well as locate chapters and verses; Bible dictionaries; commentaries written by biblical scholars;

and Bible study and teaching guides. The Internet is also an amazing resource for questions and answers related to the Bible. I highly recommend participating in a Bible study/discussion group, a seminar, or a workshop to experience insights and inspiration when learning from others. Here is a suggestion for reading difficult-to-understand passages in the Bible: Simply write in the margin: "awaiting further light." I learned this from a seminary professor who could not answer a Bible question by a student. His response: "Since I do not know the meaning of that verse, let's mark it with 'awaiting further light' and perhaps the answer will come later."

Year after year the Bible has the honor of being one of the most frequently purchased books for gifts, libraries, and coffee tables; yet surveys show that the Bible is also one of the least read books. This truth is displayed on the highly popular TV game show *Jeopardy*. Very few of the contestants do well on a Bible category. Today's preachers cannot assume their congregations know very much about the Bible, even though there are abundant resources in addressing biblical illiteracy. Christian denominations have published a multitude of study books and courses to encourage wider Bible reading, understanding, and appreciation. Gideons International, founded in 1899, has been placing complimentary Bibles in hotels and motels since 1908. Quietly working behind the scenes, Gideons today rarely gets front-page publicity related to their worldwide distribution of Bibles.[22]

I am reminded of the time, a few hours before one of my grandchildren was born, when I waited with our family in the hospital visitors room, eagerly anticipating the birth. Picking up a copy of the Bible near the magazine rack, the other grandfather read on the flyleaf, "Placed by The Gideons." He said to me, "What is a Gideon? I see these Bibles in every hotel I have stayed. Have you ever seen a Gideon?" "Yes," I responded, "in fact several men in the church I pastor are active Gideons." This led to a lively conversation about this laymen-led Bible promotion and distribution organization who took their name from Gideon in the Book of Judges.

The majority of Bible readers are looking primarily for chapter and verse information: Noah's ark and the rainbow, Ten Commandments, Golden Rule, the Good Samaritan story, and other parables told by Jesus. Reading the Bible from cover to cover or taking an academic course in "Literature of the Bible" can yield an abundance of information, but does that have a lasting influence on the reader? People open their Bibles for many reasons: some to read a verse or two in a devotional guide; others may be searching for a scripture that supports personal opinion. All who open their Bibles may be looking for information from time to time. Information is good and certainly can be helpful. But consider another approach called formational Bible reading. Whereas informational Bible reading is an exercise of the mind, formational Bible reading is oriented toward listening with one's heart and soul, allowing the verses to make a personal impact.

Formational Bible reading:

- ◆ focuses on small portions of scripture.
- ◆ is not concerned with covering an entire chapter or book.
- ◆ does not hurry.
- ◆ uncovers multiple layers of meaning.
- ◆ allows the scripture to address the reader.
- ◆ assumes a listening mode.
- ◆ is humble, open-minded, spiritually alert.
- ◆ is a spiritual discipline.

Formational Bible readers take seriously this affirmation by the Apostle Paul:

"All scripture is inspired by God and is useful for teaching, for showing mistakes, for correction, and for training character, so that the person who belongs to God can be equipped to do everything that is good" (2 Timothy 3:16-17 CEB).

Formational Bible reading asks questions of the text:

> What does this passage tell me about God?

> What does it tell me about others?

> What does it tell me about myself?

> What is God saying to me in this passage?

One time-tested way of doing formational reading and listening to God is called "lectio divina." A divine and human dialogue is desired, while listening with unhurried expectation, allowing at least 30 minutes. Here is how it works in four movements:

1. Reading or "lectio"...Begin by quieting yourself and offering prayer to center your spirit on the Holy Spirit. Then select a scripture passage. Read through it slowly at least twice, silently or aloud.
2. Reflecting or "meditatio"...Meditate on God's word and listen. Enter this scripture text with imagination and openness. Search for insights, applications, and relevant meanings. Seek to hear what God wants to communicate to you.
3. Response or "oratio"...Enter into a prayerful dialogue with God, feeling and listening for what God may be saying. We speak and God responds. God speaks and we respond.
4. Resting or "contemplation"...Contemplative prayer moves from conversation with God to communion with God. We

relax and wait and listen. Here we simply rest in God's presence.

At first, praying this way may seem a bit complicated. Just remember the four "R's" (reading, reflecting, responding, resting).[23]

Here is an example of what happened to me one day when I followed the "lectio divina" pattern. The setting is my private room at the monastery in the village of Trappist, Kentucky, called Gethsemani Abbey.[24] I had decided to go there for a three-day retreat in December 2014 following the death of my wife in October. I had been married for 58 years, and my grief was fresh and heavy. I needed some time away to sort things out and begin to consider moving on in life. After unpacking and getting settled, I opened my Bible for some solitude, silence, and scripture reading. Turning to the Book of Psalms, I read the First Psalm, a brief passage of only six verses. I had read this psalm countless times in the past with the understanding that it serves as an introduction to the Book of Psalms.

So there I sat at a small desk in my plainly furnished room, Bible in hand with notebook and pen nearby. The Common English Bible (CEB) has been my primary scripture source since it was published in 2011. Starting with prayer, I thanked God for safe travel, the privilege of being a guest at this monastery, and for anything related to my life in Psalm 1. When I got to the third verse, one word seemed to leap off the page and stopped me from reading further.

Psalm 1:3: "They are like a tree replanted by streams of water, which bears fruit at just the right time and whose leaves do not fade."

In the past I had learned this psalm, as translated in the King James Version and the New Revised Standard Version, with verse 3 reading,

"They are like trees planted by streams of water."

I promptly started questioning this word "planted." Planted and replanted are not quite the same. Which one is correct? With a growing curiosity I located the monastery library, found a concordance of the Bible, and checked out the Hebrew word behind the English translation. There it was. The Hebrew word "shathal" can be rendered in English as: plant, replant, transplant, relocate, resettle. This means plant and replant are both correct.

Returning to my room, I wrote in my journal, "Am I like a tree that is being replanted. Am I being transplanted? Is my life in a transition of moving away from familiar territory to parts unknown, from having a beloved companion for most of my life to living alone? This does have a feeling of being uprooted and moved." After I pondered the implications of all that, other thoughts started emerging. "Yes, I think I am being replanted, but I do not need to flounder in my grief because Psalm 1 also says this transplanted tree will have plenty of nourishment from streams of water and will bear fruit."

As I meditated on that thought, another journal entry: "Even though I am uncertain about my future, I know I can draw on the Living Water of Jesus every day. I can drink, absorb, take in this life-giving water that will lead to growth, health, and new life." This thought was prompted by the conversation between Jesus and the Samaritan woman at the well: Jesus said, "Everyone who drinks this (well) water, will be thirsty again, but whoever drinks from the water that I will give will never be thirsty again. The water that I give will become in those who drink it a spring of water that bubbles up into eternal life" (John 4:13-14 CEB).

Then, my prayer response: "This day, Divine and Wise Planter, my Lord and my God, keep me sensitive to your guiding presence and help me draw from the nourishing, spiritual water surrounding me here at Gethsemani Abbey and wherever I go when I leave here. Let it flow. Let me grow just like the replanted tree in Psalm 1... Thank you. Amen."

This was followed by a quiet, restful time relaxing in the peace of God that is beyond human understanding. One of the blessings of reading a portion of the Bible every day is to discover new meanings in passages that spoke in a different way in the past. Life moves on like a flowing river, with today's challenges and situations different from yesterday's. The Bible is often called the word of God, implying that these printed sentences have the potential of inspiring, motivating, guiding, forgiving, and inviting the reader to move beyond self-centered living and into a God-centered life.

When Jesus was asked to name the greatest and first commandment, he quoted Deuteronomy 6:4 and Leviticus 19:18 in the Hebrew scriptures:

"You shall love the Lord your God with all your heart, with all your being (soul), with all your mind, and with all your strength. The second is this. You shall love your neighbor as yourself. There is no other commandment greater than these" (Mark 12:30-31 NRSV).

This heart and essence of The Holy Bible challenges the reader to act, to live, to behave in God's way. As Rev. Don Bartow puts it: "An ounce of obedience is worth a ton of Bible study."[25]

A PRAYER FOR UNDERSTANDING AND INSPIRATION WHEN READING AND STUDYING THE BIBLE, BASED ON PSALM 119:105 RSV.

Gracious and loving God, as the psalmist proclaimed, so do I affirm,

"Thy word is a lamp to my feet and a light to my path." For the privilege of reading and studying your word, I am truly thankful. Should I come across verses that seem somewhat baffling and beyond my understanding, I ask for the Holy Spirit to give me patience, perseverance, and enlightenment. As I open my Bible, this is my prayer in the Name of the living Word Jesus Christ. Amen.

QUESTIONS TO PONDER

1. What is your earliest remembrance of the Bible? When did you start reading the Bible? Who encouraged you to read the Bible? Can you share other Bible-related memories?

2. Recall the last time you read from your Bible. Do you remember what it said? What did it prompt you to think or to do? Do you have a plan to read and meditate on scripture with regularity?

3. If you were to engage in "lectio divina" (reading, reflecting, responding, relaxing) what would you need to do in preparation for unhurried time, solitude, silence, and formational Bible reading?

4. What does this quotation by Thomas à Kempis (c.1380–1471) say to you?

   "Our own curiosity often hinders us in reading the Scriptures, because we wish to understand and argue when we should simply read on with humility, simplicity, and faith."

Chapter 5

SALVATION AND BEING SAVED

Jesus to Zacchaeus: "Today salvation has come to this house. For the Son came to seek and to save the lost."
(Luke 19:9-10 NRSV)

Question: Even though I have been a church member all my life, how do I know if I am saved?

Reflection: This sincere question by a 95-year-old parishioner has been voiced time and again by many older Christians and deserves more than a quick response. We begin with some biblical descriptions and definitions. The New Testament Greek word "soteria" can be translated in English: rescue, deliver, preserve, make whole, health, salvation. The Greek word "sozo" can be rendered heal, preserve, make whole, save. In the Zacchaeus story both Greek words are found in the original text: "Today soteria (salvation) has come to this house. For the Son of man (Jesus) came to seek and to sozo (save) the lost." No doubt Zacchaeus remembered that life-changing day for the rest of his life.

Countless numbers of Christians today have also had remarkable conversion experiences, turning away from old ways to new beginnings, by coming to Jesus with a repentant heart and a humble attitude. However, there are great numbers of Christians whose spiritual journey is less dramatic, yet genuinely sincere and authentic.

Before going further with the reality and process of personal salvation, it might be well to see the bigger picture from God's point of view. The Bible, cover to cover, is the record of salvation history, a primary story with dozens of subplots. The biblical narrative reveals God's eternal love for all creation and God's saving actions when humanity did not respond with love to God and love for other human beings. The creation story summarizes God's magnificent initiative: "God saw everything he had made: it was supremely good" (Genesis 1:3 CEB).

Author Richard Rohr calls this God's Plan A, "original goodness" for Adam and Eve and all of creation. The Garden of Eden provided health, welfare, blessings upon blessings, and a personal relationship with God. This was the divine intention, a round-the-clock state of well-being, a perpetual environment of joyful living. But the plot not only thickened; it got sick and dark. Enter human disobedience to God, hence Plan B, which addresses sinful humanity and the so-called "original sin."[26]

But God, who never gives up on the human race, devised ways to encourage wayward people to return to Plan A, "original goodness." Some of God's many attempts to turn humankind around and head in the right direction: First came a new beginning for humanity via Noah's family, saved on the ark and sealed with the promise of the rainbow; later Abraham was called by God to develop and lead a great nation called Hebrews, promising, "I will bless you and by you all the families of the earth will be blessed" (Genesis 12:1-4 NRSV).

Abraham remained faithful throughout his long life, yet not all in the family followed his example. Years later, when through a series of unfortunate circumstances the Hebrew people were enslaved in Egypt, God raised up another charismatic leader named Moses, who on the way to the "Promised Land" was given the Ten Commandments. These laws provided divine instructions for putting God first in all things and living respectfully and morally toward all human beings. This seemed to work out for a generation or two; then sinful disobedience arose and halted the forward progress, a pattern often repeated in Israel's checkered history. In an effort to put the brakes on this backsliding, God raised up spokespersons who boldly condemned the nation's unacceptable behavior and proclaimed a return to God's righteousness. We call these courageous persons "prophets" and note their names in the titles of several Old Testament books. Even though some people did respond with faithfulness to God's saving love and mercy, the overwhelming majority of the population did not. So it was, according to the salvation history of the Bible, that God tried once more to communicate directly with humanity.

"In the past, God spoke through the prophets to our ancestors in many times and many ways. In these final days, though, he spoke to us through a Son" (Hebrews 1:1-2 CEB).

According to historians, there is absolutely no doubt that some 2,000 years ago, a man named Jesus of Nazareth lived in Palestine. He attracted Jews and Gentiles with his wise teachings and miraculous signs. He referred often to his Heavenly Father and even though he respected and cared for all people, after a brief public ministry, he was condemned and crucified. Those who followed him were called Christians and continued to follow him after he died.[27]

With these "bare bones" facts in mind, we turn to the Gospel of John for another view of Jesus, one that goes way back in time before Planet Earth was created.

> "In the beginning was the Word and the Word was with God and the Word was God… Everything came into being through the Word, and without the Word nothing came into being. The Word became flesh and made his home among us. We have seen his glory, like that of a father's only son, full of grace and truth" (John 1:1-14 CEB).

We often refer to the Bible as the word of God (small "w"), meaning God communicates to readers through inspired, written words of many authors. Whereas Word of God (capital "W") proclaims boldly and plainly that the creating Word took the form of a human baby and without political or royal fanfare was born to peasant parents in the small village of Bethlehem. We refer to this significant event as the Incarnation (enfleshment) of the Word, sometimes called "the mother of all birthdays," celebrated the world over every year at Christmastime.

So, was Jesus 50 percent divine and 50 percent human? The creeds of the church do not speak with one voice on this question. Traditional Christianity simply names Jesus as the Second Person of the Holy Trinity (Father, Son, Holy Spirit); however, it is clear by reading the four Gospels (Matthew, Mark, Luke, John) that Jesus always saw himself in a subordinate role to his Heavenly Father, to whom he prayed fervently and frequently. Furthermore, even though Jesus closely identified himself with his Father, he never called himself "God." Jesus is quite clear about this in his conversation with his disciple Philip, who requested, "Lord, show us the Father: that will be enough for us." Jesus replied, "Whoever has seen me has seen the Father. I am in the

Father and the Father is in me… The words that I have spoken to you I don't speak on my own. The Father who dwells in me does his works. Trust me when I say I am in the Father and the Father is in me" (John 14:8-11 CEB).

Because of his wisdom, his ability to speak with an uncanny authority when confronted by his opposition, along with his genuine love for marginalized and common people, Jesus drew huge crowds wherever he went. This caused a leader of the Jews named Nicodemus to come to Jesus under the cover of darkness with "theological questions." This conversation between two teachers (rabbis) is recorded in John 3:1-21 CEB. Focus on verse 3: "Very truly I tell you, no one can see the Kingdom of God without being born from above (born again, born anew)."

Nicodemus totally misunderstood Jesus and thought he meant another physical birth. Not so, says Jesus. Think "spiritual birth." When someone raises the questions, "Am I saved?" or "How can I be saved?" there seems to be a conscious and persistent idea that the way of salvation has something to do with that ancient dialogue between Jesus and Nicodemus. As I have heard it voiced, "I am a born-again Christian. Are you?"

Now take a closer look at these often quoted words in John's Gospel:

"For God so loved the world that he gave his only Son, so that every one who believes in him may not perish but have eternal life. Indeed God did not send the Son into the world to condemn the world, but in order that the world might be saved through him" (John 3:16-17 CEB).

Notice there is no timeline between believing in the Son and experiencing eternal life. My interpretation is that eternal life began for me the moment I accepted Jesus and committed my life to follow him.

No waiting until physical death of the body to experience, as the hymn goes, "a foretaste of glory divine."[28] Later on in John 5:24 CEB, Jesus repeats and clarifies, "I assure you that whoever hears my word and believes in the one who sent me has eternal life and won't come under judgment but has passed from death into life." And again Jesus reinforces this teaching: "I am the bread of life. I assure you, whoever believes in me has eternal life" (John 6:47-48 CEB).

These verses also say that God, our Creator, has no favorites, but loves all of the people of all the nations on this planet. Why? So that everyone might have the opportunity to be saved (experience salvation) through his Son. And how does one know if he or she is saved? The short answer: the decision to accept and follow Jesus results in a lifetime of positive changes (some small and some large) in attitudes, understandings, and behaviors. Several years ago some of the people who made a personal commitment to Jesus at a Billy Graham Crusade in New York City were interviewed and asked what differences that had made. Responded one woman who was employed in the housekeeping department of a large hotel: "Well, for one thing, I no longer sweep the dirt under the rugs."

Jesus is God's answer to humanity's habit of looking at life through self-centered, self-oriented lenses. The way to experience a return to "original goodness" (God's Plan A) is to believe and trust in Jesus (Plan B). Result: eternal life beginning immediately. But what about the problem of sin? An angel appeared to Joseph in a dream with this amazing message: "Mary will give birth to a son, and you will call him Jesus (one who saves) because he will save his people from their sins" (Matthew 1:21 CEB). We do not have to search for God. Instead, God searches for us. God loves us just the way we are and offers forgiveness, grace, mercy, and love in and through Jesus. This ever-searching God has been called "The Hound of Heaven," who is in a continuous hunt for human response. Salvation, then, is a gift from God to be received or rejected.

Think of the various ways Christians have said yes and accepted the gift of God's salvation in Jesus. Some would point to a special time of going forward in a church service when the pastor issued an altar call to accept Jesus as Lord and Savior; some might recall a summer evening when attending church camp as a teenager and making their faith commitment; some have met their Savior in prison while serving time for criminal behavior. Something we read in a book, or see in a movie, or hear in a song may cause us to rethink our life and turn our attention to Jesus. Some come to church membership or confirmation classes and after study and instructions make a public commitment to be a lifelong disciple of Jesus. Several years ago the famous missionary to India, E. Stanley Jones, wrote a book with the one-word title: EVANGELISM. When I read that book as a seminary student, I discovered within its pages 300 short stories of how people came to know and accept Jesus. What an eye-opener that was, as I began to see the creativity of God's Spirit working in the world. To hold the position that there is only one church, one way, or one creed is to overlook the countless ways God's saving love reaches out to all humanity.

I recall an illustration in this book focusing on two widely different experiences of what it means to be saved. Picture yourself in a completely darkened room. Outside, the sun is radiantly shining. Inside, you are sitting in total darkness. Suddenly a window shade rolls all the way to the top and the sun floods the room with a brilliant light. This could be a metaphor illustrating instant, dramatic conversion from a life lived in darkness to a welcomed light giving new life (born again). The other way of receiving the light in this darkened room is for the shade to raise only an inch every now and then. Light comes in but not all at once. As the shade slowly but deliberately keeps rising year after year, more and more light flows in until the room is completely enveloped in light. This describes the Christian whose spiritual growth takes a more gradual and sincere path in changing, converting, and knowing God's love as revealed in Jesus Christ.

I thank God for those Christians who can name the place, date, and time when the window shades of their souls dramatically went from totally closed to fully open and the grace of God flooded their entire being. Interestingly, in conversation with those who claim this experience, I have discovered that prior to that unique moment, the Holy Spirit had been quietly working behind the scenes, planting the seeds of salvation. Perhaps all Christians would agree with the man who, although he could not pinpoint a dramatic moment in his life when he first knew the reality of God's love, said it all began around the year 33 AD, when the innocent Jesus died on a cross and three days later was known to be resurrected and alive. Yes, that catalytic weekend changed the course of history and made it possible for all who believe in and follow Jesus to have a spiritual rebirth, born from above.

The word most often used to describe what happens in the Christian's life is "conversion," meaning "to turn." As a seminary professor expressed it: "Christian conversion is a lifelong process. The first thing to be converted to Jesus is one's heart, and the last thing surrendered is usually one's checkbook." Because basic human nature is self-centered and egotistically oriented, the spiritual journey is not a smooth path. To quote the Apostle Paul, "All have sinned and fall short of the glory of God" (Romans 3:23 CEB).

Yet, by the grace, mercy, forgiveness, and love of God, life changes and spiritual growth does happen to Christians. Here is a list of comments I have received from several persons who shared their experiences and answers to the questions: What does salvation mean to you? How do you know if you are saved? What does it mean for you that Jesus is your Lord and Savior? (related biblical verses have been added to these personal responses).

1. I am saved from unnecessary anxiety and distress by knowing the peace of God even in the midst of life's troubling, tragic moments. (Philippians 4:7)
2. I am saved from a non-caring attitude toward others to offering encouragement and comfort in times of stress and discouragement. (2 Corinthians 1:3-5)
3. I am saved from bypassing and forgetting about God each day to adopting and practicing prayer as a lifestyle. (Philippians 4:6)
4. I am saved from lack of participation to increasing appreciation for Holy Communion.(I Corinthians 11:23-26)
5. I am saved from the desire to accumulate more and more "stuff" to rethinking priorities and values in life. As a woman shared in a spiritual retreat: "If your security in life depends on things that can be taken away, you are living on the false edge of security." (Luke 12:13-21)
6. I am saved from ignoring God to meeting regularly with my church community to praise and worship God. As the counselor suggested to a client who seemed totally involved with herself, "I strongly recommend that you take a trip to Niagara Falls and when you arrive simply gaze at something bigger than yourself." (Psalm 145)
7. I am saved from holding grudges and resentment to giving and receiving forgiveness in maintaining healthy relationships. (Ephesians 4:31-32)
8. I am saved from giving in to tempting situations to having spiritual help in resisting temptation. (Hebrews 2:18)

This, of course, is not an exhaustive list of positive changes, but it gives some examples of what can and often does happen in the lives of those who say "yes" to Jesus. As the Apostle Paul wrote: "Work out your own salvation with fear and trembling. For it is God who is at work in you, enabling you both to will and to work for his good pleasure" (Philippians 2:12-13 CEB).

Paul is not saying that we obtain salvation by our personal good works; rather, he is giving God the credit for initiating the desire within us to want to live changed and changing lives. This verse in Paul's Letter to the Ephesians is the heart of the matter: "For by grace you have been saved through faith, and this is not your own doing; it is the gift of God, not the result of works, so that no one may boast. For we are what he has made us, created in Christ Jesus for good works, which God prepared beforehand to be our way of life" (Ephesians 2:8-10 NRSV).

From the moment we claim Jesus Christ as Lord and Savior, we receive the gift of salvation. Then we spend the rest of our lives figuring out, working out, living out the consequences, challenges, and blessings of that personal commitment. God working inward; human beings working outward. That is the New Testament formula for being saved (an ongoing process). Recall Jesus meeting Zacchaeus in the opening of this chapter. Read the entire story in Luke 19:1-10 and notice the sequence: Something was prompting and encouraging Zacchaeus to seek out Jesus. I call that "something" God's Holy Spirit. They met face-to-face. Next Zacchaeus (the crooked tax collector) repented (turned around) by admitting his corruptness, pledged to make amends, and offered to repay what he owed to his community. At that point in the story, Jesus says, "Today salvation has come to this household."

We sometimes hear or read about persons who rejected God's gift of salvation for many years, but then made a deathbed confession and accepted Jesus Christ. On the other hand, I have never known of anyone during their final moments who uttered any regrets for being a Christian throughout their life. The Gospel, as summarized in John 3:16-17, is freely offered, but not mandated. To some it may seem too good to be true, and they seek other ways to satisfy their spirituality. To others, the life and teachings of Jesus are appealing and admirable, but are rejected as being beyond explanation and rational understanding.

Perhaps the most practical path to knowing Jesus is best expressed in this thought-provoking word from the heart and soul of Dr. Albert Schweitzer.

"He comes to us as One unknown, without a name, as of old, by the lakeside. He came to those men who knew him not. He speaks to us the same word, 'Follow thou me!' and sets us to the tasks which He has to fulfill for our time. He commands. And to those who obey Him, whether they be wise or simple, He will reveal Himself in the toils, the conflicts, the sufferings which they shall pass through in His fellowship, and, as an ineffable (indescribable) mystery, they shall learn in their own experience who He is."[29]

QUESTIONS TO PONDER

1. After reading this chapter what questions arose in your mind? You may want to discuss these with a Christian friend or minister.

2. To Christian readers of this book: Can you name some of the seeds planted by the Holy Spirit before you made your personal decision to accept and follow Jesus Christ?

3. What is your personal understanding of "salvation" and "being saved"?

4. Referring to the list of personal statements about "being saved," what would you add?

Chapter 6

BAD FRIDAY/GOOD FRIDAY

*"The message of the cross…is the power of
God for those who are being saved."*
(I Corinthians 1:18 CEB)

QUESTION: Why do we call the day Jesus died on the cross Good Friday? It was a horribly Bad Friday for Jesus.

REFLECTION: The story is told about a young boy who, as he grew, developed a noticeably odd way of walking. He leaned to one side. Doctors put him through a battery of tests but found no cause, no scoliosis, no muscular abnormality. Then one day a strange thing happened. The boy's father walked into the doctor's office leaning obviously to one side. "Why do you walk like that?" asked the physician. "Well, Doc, it's like this," he responded. "Several years ago I lost a couple toes in a mower accident." The doctor concluded that the son walked off-kilter because his dad walked that way.[30]

Is it so strange that the young boy assumed his father's example was the model for him to follow without question? Yet, countless numbers of Sunday School bred Christians grew up not questioning the death of Jesus on a cross. Then there are those who admire and respect Jesus, but simply cannot believe how the death of this innocent man centuries ago could have any benefit or connection for people living today. I am inviting you to have a conversation framed by these questions:

1. What does the Bible say about the issues that led to the crucifixion?
2. Did Jesus have a choice about his death on a cross?
3. What do we mean by "theories of atonement"?
4. Was it God's will and plan even before Jesus was born that God's beloved Son would experience death by crucifixion?

FIRST QUESTION: What does the Bible say about the issues that led to the crucifixion? For the answer to this question, we first put the spotlight on the environmental factors. During the time of Jesus, there were many people who would have felt better if he had not been around. His teaching, preaching, and lifestyle gave birth to opposition from religious and political groups of his day. The religious establishment (dating back to the time of Moses and the giving of the Ten Commandments) consisted of Pharisees, who were considered the defenders of Israel's ancient faith and the authoritative interpreters of religious Law. One of their main charges against Jesus was his intentional lack of observing the strict rules of the Sabbath. Then there were the aristocrats of the Jewish nation called Sadducees, who tended to be more conservative than the Pharisees when issues arose over interpretation of the Law, believing they were the true keepers of their faith tradition. In the interest of peace and harmony, the Sadducees cooperated with the Roman authorities, giving them a political voice. Among the other parties vying for attention were the so-called Zealots or Zionists, whose goal was to overthrow the Romans by military force. These rebels were the guerrilla-freedom fighters of that day, believing that their way was the only way to restore the nation of Israel. Something Mark Twain said aptly applies to the first century as well as the 21st century: "Man is the only animal that has the true religion...all of them."

Jesus tried to divorce himself from the Zealots and their cause. He did not want to be identified as a national hero or another King David. Notice that the opposition forces worked openly, as well as behind the scenes, to eliminate Jesus from the very beginning of his public ministry. The Gospel of Mark forecasts the early demise of Jesus. After he violated a Sabbath rule by healing a man with a withered hand, the Pharisees got together with the supporters of Herod to plan how to destroy Jesus (Mark 3:1-6 CEB).

When the religious leaders saw an opportunity to erase Jesus from the scene, they took him to the Roman Governor Pontius Pilate, requesting the death penalty based on three trumped-up charges:

1. forbidding the tax payment to Caesar;
2. speaking and acting against the better interest of the Jewish people;
3. claiming to be a king.

Even though the four Gospels differ slightly in the details when Jesus appeared in Pilate's court, they all agree that Pilate believed Jesus was innocent and intended to set him free. This was totally unacceptable to the religious leadership who incited the crowd to shout, "Crucify him! Crucify him!" Pilate caved in, rationalizing that the popularity of Jesus could pose a threat to his authority, and ordered the death of Jesus on a cross bearing the sign: Jesus King of the Jews.

SECOND QUESTION: Did Jesus have a choice about his death on a cross?

We can only guess how Jesus felt about his cross, even though he did mention this more than once to his disciples. Some Christians would simply point to their red-letter editions of the New Testament that have all the words of Jesus printed with red ink. However, it is nearly impossible to separate his authentic words from the recalled memories of the early Church (first and second century Christians). Some biblical scholars say that Mark's Gospel was written around 55 AD, and that John's Gospel could have been put into writing as late as 75 years after Jesus died. Who can remember what was said a year ago, let alone many years in the past? This makes it difficult and likely impossible to separate the words that the early Christians passed on about Jesus and what Jesus actually said.

Nevertheless, taking the utterances of Jesus at face value, he clearly spoke more than once of his impending, early death. Naturally this upset the twelve Apostles, who tried to steer Jesus away from Jerusalem, the headquarters of the opposition forces. Jesus took the Twelve aside and told them, "Look, we are going up to Jerusalem. The Son of Man (meaning Jesus himself) will be handed over to the chief priests and legal experts. They will condemn him to death. They will hand him over to the Gentiles to be ridiculed, tortured, and crucified. But he will be raised on the third day" (Matthew 20:17-19 CEB). On the day we now call Palm Sunday, Jesus staged a parade into the city of Jerusalem, evoking praises from the onlookers: "Hosanna to the Son of David. Blessings on the one who comes in the name of the Lord" (Matthew 21:9 CEB).

Then Jesus did something that he knew would provoke anger and controversy. He entered the Temple and after surveying what was going on, Jesus intentionally overturned tables of the merchants and rebuked those who were taking advantage of the pilgrims who had come to observe the annual Passover in Jerusalem. He ordered them to stop desecrating the Temple. Buying and selling, exchanging money, hawking sacrificial animals was a huge business, a corrupt enterprise in those days. A case can be made that Jesus was condemned to die, not so much for religious reasons, but because he disrupted dealing and trading, thus potentially upsetting the economy of Jerusalem.

Throughout the next several days (called Holy Week), Jesus continued his public ministry (teaching, preaching, and healing). Then on Thursday evening, following the Passover meal with the Apostles (now called The Last Supper), Jesus went to the Gethsemane Garden to pray about his next steps. A portion of this memorable prayer is quoted for us to consider.

"My Father, if it's possible, take this cup of suffering away from me. However, not what I want but what you want" (Matthew 26:39 CEB).

He knew his enemies were closing in. Jesus did not want to die on a cross. How else can one explain his excruciating agony at that point in his life. He was fully human, full of life, full of dreams, full of hope, full of love, and only 33 years old. Did Jesus have a choice? Yes, I believe he did. Could he have escaped and gone into exile with his disciples? I think he had that option. Nevertheless, Jesus yielded to a higher authority, his heavenly Father, and cooperated with the horrible events that followed. The next day, on that very bad Friday around 3:00 p.m., the tortured, pain-racked, crucified Jesus cried out these soul-wrenching words: "My God, my God, why have you forsaken me?" (Mark 15:34 CEB). Then followed by, "Father, into your hands I commend my spirit" (Luke 23:46 NRSV). And he breathed his last breath.

THIRD QUESTION: What do we mean by "theories of atonement"?

In the centuries following Jesus' death on a cross, the word most frequently used in attempting to explain the crucifixion is "atonement." A theory is designed to help us comprehend what appears to be beyond our limited understanding. The word "atonement" as it is used in the Bible has several English translations. As recorded in the New Testament, atonement (think at-one-ment) means restored harmony and reconciliation of God and humanity. When asked why Jesus was crucified, it is likely that the majority of Christians would consider it a "no-brainer" to simply respond: "Jesus died for my sins." After all, check out the third verse in the popular hymn "How Great Thou Art."

> And when I think that God, his Son not sparing;
> Sent him to die, I scarce can take it in;
> That on the cross, my burden gladly bearing,
> He bled and died to take away my sins.[31]

Keep in mind that the four Gospels and the Letters of Paul do not speak with one voice, but offer a variety of interpretations concerning atonement. Here are a few of the atonement theories.

RANSOM THEORY: This was the main explanation for the first one thousand years of church history and held that Jesus' death was kind of a transaction between God and the devil. To release the devil's hold on humanity, Jesus paid the full price and achieved supreme and eternal victory over sin and death. As recorded in Mark 10:45 NRSV, "The son of man came not to be served but to serve, and to give his life as a ransom for many." By placing our faith in Jesus Christ, we too share in his victory over sin and death. However, the devil was tricked by God, whose trump card was the resurrection of Jesus three days later.

SUBSTITUTION THEORY: This widely held theory throughout Christianity today says that Christ did for us what we could not do for ourselves; namely, pay our sin debt to God. By taking our sins and the sins of the world upon himself, Christ satisfied divine justice. Paul proclaimed in his Letter to the Romans: "God shows his love for us, because while we were still sinners Christ died for us. So, now that we have been made righteous by his blood, we can be even more certain that we will be saved from God's wrath through him" (Romans 5:8-9).

MORAL INFLUENCE THEORY: Christ's death on a cross serves as the ultimate example for us to lead lives of sacrificial love. This concept emphasizes not a wrathful, vengeful God, but a merciful, forgiving, loving God who took the initiative through his special son, Jesus, to reach out to all humanity. Reflect on these words of Jesus: "When I am lifted up from the earth, I will draw every one to me" (John 12:32-33 CEB). He said this to show how he was going to die. This is also called the Magnet Theory of atonement because the life, message, mission, and cross of Jesus continue to be attractions and blessings.

Other theories of atonement abound, including The Victory Model, The Divinity Model, and The Mirror Model.[32] So what is one to make of these many attempted explanations? We can conclude that there is some truth in each theory. Yet, no single one is able to thoroughly clarify and make plain for human understanding this divine mystery surrounding the cross of Jesus. My hope is that those who read this book will give serious thought to these various theories and formulate their own understanding. Consider this wise comment by Richard Rohr:

"The cross is not the price that Jesus had to pay to talk God into loving us. It is simply where love will lead us. Jesus names the agenda. If we love, if we give ourselves to feel the pain of the world, it will crucify us. This understanding of the crucifixion is much better than thinking of Jesus as paying some debt to an alienated God who needs to be talked into loving us."[33]

Rohr feels strongly that Jesus did not come to change the mind of God about humanity. Jesus came to change the mind of humanity about God.

FOURTH QUESTION: Was it God's will and plan, even before Jesus was born, that God's beloved Son would experience death by crucifixion? The English author and minister of the 20th century, Leslie Weatherhead, has this understanding of God's will:

- The Intentional Will of God: These are God's ideal desires and benevolent yearnings for all human beings.
- The Circumstantial Will of God: Within changing circumstances due to human free-will, God continues to be present, involved, and concerned.
- The Ultimate Will of God: The purposes and yearnings of God are finally accomplished.
- In applying this concept to the cross, Weatherhead goes on to say, "It was not the intentional will of God, surely, that Jesus should be crucified, but that Jesus would be followed. If the people in Jesus' day had received and understood his message, repented of their sins, and welcomed the Kingdom of God, the history of the world would have been different. The crucifixion was the will of evil-minded men, not the will of God. But when Jesus was faced with the situation brought on by his opposition, he dealt with the dilemma of running away or being crucified. It was in this sense that Jesus prayed, 'Father, remove this cup from me; yet, not what I want but what you want'"[34] (Mark 14:36 CEB).

Even though God's intentional will concerning Jesus had been thwart-ed, God used those ugly circumstances to move forward. Three days later came the Resurrection, thus paving the way for God's ultimate will to be fully realized. This is the message Christians celebrate every Easter Sunday. No one, no thing, no evil can defeat God.

"We know that all things work together for good for those who love God, who are called according to his purpose" (Romans 8:28 NRSV).

Around age 30, Jesus launched his public ministry with a positive attitude and a hopeful future. Through his instructive parables and healing ministry, Jesus attracted great crowds of people. His Heavenly Father fully expected Jesus to be believed, accepted, and followed. For instance: At his baptism: Came a voice from heaven, "You are my Son, the Beloved; with you I am well pleased" (Luke 3:22 NRSV).

This same message was sounded from heaven when Jesus and three disciples gathered on a high mountain (The Transfiguration). "This is my Son whom I dearly love. I am very pleased with him. Listen to him" (Matthew 17:5 CEB).

However, as his enemies' intentions and actions became bolder, Jesus shared more sober and solemn messages with his disciples. Weatherhead, in his book *A Plain Man Looks at the Cross*, gives our inquiring minds an insightful quotation.

"The words of Jesus about his suffering and death reveal that he will-ingly committed himself to some mighty task, costly to him beyond our imagining, but effecting for all people a deliverance beyond their own power to achieve, and that in doing so, he knew himself to be utterly and completely one with God the Father."[35]

This is why that horribly bad Friday has been named Good Friday.

When gazing upon the cross, the most iconic symbol in Christianity the world over, Christians know in their heart and soul what the mind cannot fully understand, that the crucified Jesus truly is Lord and Savior. I believe Jesus died not fully realizing that his death would provide the way for humanity to experience atonement, reconciliation, forgiveness, and salvation. His prayer in Gethsemane Garden reveals that Jesus had hoped there would be some other way. I only wish there had been some other way. Without doubt, his Heavenly Father preferred some other way. However, if God had only wanted a sacrifice on that cross, Jesus would have stayed dead. But he didn't and that's the focus of the next chapter in this book.

QUESTIONS TO PONDER

1. Do you have a personal theory of atonement? If not try to write a brief statement that you could share with another person.

2. Why is it that Good Friday Services are not as well attended as Palm Sunday and Easter Sunday church services?

3. Can you apply Weatherhead's three actions of God's will (intentional, circumstantial, and ultimate) to any situation in your life's experiences?

4. In a church hymnal locate Isaac Watts' profound hymn "When I Survey the Wondrous Cross." Taking some unhurried time and reflecting on the verses, what questions, thoughts, insights come to mind?

Chapter 7

---—∞—---

LIFE AFTER LIFE

Jesus said to Martha: "I am the resurrection and
the life. Whoever believes in me will live, even
though they die. Everyone who lives and believes
in me will never die. Do you believe this?"
(John 11: 25-26 CEB)

QUESTIONS: Is this life all there is? What does the Bible say about an afterlife? What evidence do we have of an afterlife?

REFLECTIONS: These kinds of questions, raised by older adults with inquiring minds, highlight a universal curiosity about the possibility of life after our present life. The scripture verses quoted above record a conversation Jesus had with Martha after her brother Lazarus died and are emphasized at memorial services of Christians. There is a universal longing or belief in life after death.

Anthropological evidence suggests that every culture has a God-given, innate sense of the eternal, that this world is not all there is.[36] But what happens after life on earth? Research reveals a wide range of concepts from very detailed descriptions of life after death based on near-death experiences and religious teachings to a vague notion but sincere hope that there truly is something more. Like the man who wrote this letter to himself when his aging and weakened body began to fail.

"When you can go no further, I shall leave you and be free. When we separate I shall continue to exist. A power greater than you and I started us on our journey. Your part is approaching its end, and you are aware of it. But my journey has merely begun, and I know it. Our separation, therefore, is not one of sadness but of joy. You are weary and want to stop. I am longing to alight from this slowing vehicle and go on without you."

Let's begin to explore the so-called "afterlife" by considering what the Bible records on this topic beginning with the words "heaven" and "heavenly," mentioned over 700 times. The Hebrew and Greek words when translated into English basically mean the same thing: lofty sky or space above the earth. The Book of Genesis 1:1-31 conveys a pre-scientific concept that the earth is flat; above the earth is a gigantic upside-down bowl; heaven is the arch-shaped horizon and sky where the sun and clouds move; when the windows of heaven open, water rains down on the earth; God dwells above and beyond the sky.

Our ever increasing knowledge of outer space labels this ancient view of the universe quite outdated. Some readers may recall the sarcastic remark made by the Russian cosmonaut who boasted that since he had flown his space ship into the heavens and did not see God, that proves the folly of religious belief in a higher power. Although some Bible references to heaven do indicate a location, other scriptures take us to another level of meaning. In the New Testament, the Gospels of Matthew, Mark, and Luke say that 40 days after Easter, Jesus ascended into heaven. The Apostles Creed states, "He arose from the dead and ascended into heaven." So, you may ask, "Where is heaven?"

The teaching and the preaching of Jesus, using stories or parables, focused on his primary message, the Kingdom of Heaven or the Kingdom of God. Recall that Jesus taught his disciples to pray, "Thy kingdom come, Thy will be done on earth as it is in heaven" (Matthew 6:10 KJV). When Jesus talked about heaven, he was not referring to a physical location, but rather to a spiritual state of continuing existence where the sovereign God reigns supreme. In the New Testament, heaven becomes synonymous with eternal life.

Today even though countless numbers of people have positive thoughts and expectations about heaven, there is some reluctance as in the quip, "Everyone wants to go to heaven, but no one wants to die." Like the story told about the preacher who one Sunday morning, after a rousing sermon on the rewards and benefits of heaven, offered this invitation to the congregation. "Now, everyone who wants to go to heaven get up, come down front, and stand with me." Story goes that nearly 100 percent of the gathered flock did that. The exception was one elderly man who stayed in his pew and did not move. Said the minister to the hold-out, "Why are you not joining the rest of us? Don't you want to go to heaven?" "Well, of course, Preacher," he responded, "but it looked to me like you were getting a load to go right now and I'm not ready."

Reflect on these selected verses from the many biblical references to heaven:

+ Heaven can mean the physical archway, the sky surrounding the Planet Earth. (Psalm 8:3)
+ In heaven our physical bodies are replaced with spiritual bodies. (1 Corinthians 15:42-44)

- In heaven we will know God completely and have all our questions answered. (1 Corinthians 13:10-12)
- Heaven is free of all pain, struggle, tears, sorrow, sin and evil. (Revelation 21:1-4)

Heaven will not be boring, but will be filled with pleasant surprises and unlimited opportunities for personal fulfillment and continued growth.

"No eye has seen, nor ear heard, nor the human heart conceived, what God has prepared for those who love him" (1 Corinthians 2:9 NRSV).

Heaven is not limited to a certain number of residents. As Jesus told his disciples, "Let not your hearts be troubled; believe in God, believe also in me. In my Father's house there are many rooms. When I go and prepare a place for you, I will come again and will take you to myself, that where I am you may be also. I am the way, the truth, and the life" (John 14:1-6 NRSV).

The concept of going to heaven is often compared to a homecoming, a reuniting of family and friends. My wife endured multiple health issues in her last year of life on earth. One afternoon during that difficult time, I saw her sitting in her favorite chair, relaxed, calm, and busily writing something. "Mary Lou, what are you doing?" I asked. With a gentle smile she looked up and said, "Oh, I'm just making a list of all the dear people I will see and be with in heaven."

Elton Trueblood, the Quaker philosopher and author, makes a powerful statement about life after life in his book *The Future of the Christian*:

"If God is like Christ, it would be illogical to assume that His concern for persons could come to an end with the death of mortal bodies.

Consequently, firm conviction about the Life Everlasting is inevitably a part of any truly evangelical faith. Insofar as we trust in the Living God, we are bound to see Him as Lord, not only of the present, but of the future as well. To the rational being it is an absurdity to suppose that the Lord of heaven and earth would, in the end, abandon those beings who, in spite of their sins, are the very jewels of His creation. If God is like Christ, it is a fair conclusion that personality will not end with our fleshly decay, but will continue and flourish in ways beyond our capacity either to ask or to think. It is not strange, therefore, that the last phrase of the Apostles' Creed says: 'And I believe in the Life Everlasting. Amen.'"[37]

In the last chapter (Bad Friday/Good Friday) our focus was on the crucifixion of Jesus. However, we must not separate Good Friday from Easter Sunday. Without the resurrection of Jesus from the grave, the Christian movement would have remained a small membership cult. But as the four-year-old girl said to her family around the Easter dinner table when asked, "What did you learn in Sunday School today?" She replied with a smiling face, "Teacher said he didn't stay dead." That is the Gospel (Good News) that our souls crave to hear. The bad news oriented world is starved for help and hope. I believe that is why churches the world over are filled to overflowing, wall to wall, with people on Easter Sundays, plus those who participate in outdoor Sunrise Services. Many Christians who rarely pay attention to church the rest of the year tend to show up on Easter.

Intricately related to the Easter message is the name "Jesus Christ." We tend to use these two words interchangeably. "Christ" is not Jesus' last name. "Christ" can be translated in Hebrew "Messiah." In the Greek "Messiah" becomes "Christ" as in "Jesus, the Christ." In Gospel of Mark 8:29 NRSV is recorded a conversation Jesus had one day with his apostles. "Who do you say that I am?" Peter answered him, "You are the Messiah" (or, the Christ). We could say that the man Jesus died on the cross, but was raised by the power of God to become the Messiah/ Christ. Richard Rohr offers an insight by calling Jesus the microcosm of God and Christ the macrocosm of God.[38] Jesus, being human, was limited to one place at a time. He never claimed to be God. However, his life and personality revealed the very heart and character of God, whom he referred to as his Heavenly Father. Hence the concept of Jesus being the microcosm of God. The Risen Christ, on the other hand, is not limited in any way and is the universal macrocosm of God. As described in the Letter to the Ephesians 1:18 CEB, "Christ is the head of the body, the church... the one who is firstborn from among the dead so that he might occupy the first place in everything." Notice we do not refer to the church as The Body of Jesus. Rather, the church is called The Body of Christ. Throughout his letters to New Testament churches, Paul speaks often of being "in Christ." In Colossians 1:27 CEB, he wrote, "Christ living in you, the hope of glory." When two Christians meet, an appropriate greeting would be: "The Christ in me greets the Christ in you and together we are one in Christ."

Returning then to the question: what evidence do we have of the possibility of life after life? Ongoing research indicates that many thousands of persons have had near-death experiences (NDE). These are people who came close to dying in a medical or non-medical setting. Many were pronounced clinically dead, but were resuscitated and lived to report their experiences. It is estimated that 5 percent of the adult American population have had a NDE. Medical, psychological, and spiritual investigations have led to hundreds of publications on this subject. Here are some common reflections.

- Confirmation that there is life outside the physical body.
- Awareness of being in the presence of family members and friends who have died.

- A common experience of light, warmth, and peace.
- Removes the fear of dying.
- Reinforces the belief that death is a transition to another life.

In the Recommended Reading section, several books are listed for those who want more data and details to explore the NDE phenomenon.

In his book *Christianity and World Religions*, Adam Hamilton expresses appreciation for certain teachings of Hinduism (transcendent glory of God), of Buddhism (detachment from material things), of Judaism (social justice and being obedient to God), and of Islam (discipline of prayer five times each day). However, he notes Christianity is unique. No other world religion claims resurrection of a deceased founder. "It is in the life, death, and resurrection of Jesus that God has definitely spoken and offered us a grace, mercy, and love that has the power to save us from our brokenness and to give us life."[39] For those whose minds continue to ask questions about the Resurrection, I highly recommend Lee Strobel's book: *The Case For Easter: A Journalist Investigates the Evidence for the Resurrection*.

For me the most believable evidence and proof that Christ arose and continues to be active today is the Church, the Body of Christ. Fifty days after Easter on Pentecost, the Church was born and within a few years moved beyond Israel to include the Gentile world. If the Christian movement depended only on human leadership, there would be no churches today. A reading of church history reveals corruption, immorality, and hypocrisy of some church leaders. But the leadership of the Risen Christ made the positive difference, and continues even to this day. Christ has kept the promise he gave to his followers immediately before ascending into heaven. "Go and make disciples of all nations, baptizing them in the name of the Father and of the Son and of the Holy Spirit, teaching them to obey everything that I've commanded you. Look, I myself will be with you every day until the end of this present age" (Matthew 28:19-20 CEB).

This entire chapter can be summarized with these uplifting words:

"May the God and Father of our Lord Jesus Christ be blessed! On account of his vast mercy, he has given us new birth. You have been born anew into a living hope through the resurrection of Jesus Christ from the dead. You have a pure and enduring inheritance that cannot perish, an inheritance that is presently kept safe in heaven for you" (1 Peter 1:3-4 CEB).

QUESTIONS TO PONDER

1. How would you describe or define heaven?

2. How do you interpret Richard Rohr's statement:

   "Jesus is the microcosm of God, and Christ is the macrocosm of God"?

3. If you could interview someone who claims to have had a near-death experience (NDE), what questions would you ask?

4. What is your understanding of this verse in the Book of Hebrews 13:8 RSV:

   "Jesus Christ is the same yesterday, today, and forever!"?

Chapter 8

STAYING HEALTHY

"Even in my old age with gray hair, do not abandon me,
O God. Do not cast me off when my strength is used up."
(Psalm 71:9,18 NRSV)

Question: Growing old isn't what I thought it would be when I retired. The aging process is hard to live with. Is staying healthy even an option at my age?

Reflection: Let's be realistic. In our advancing years, we do have more and more health issues, especially physically speaking. Our aging bodies simply do not function as well now as when we were younger. Sometimes our physical limitations slow us down to the place where we wonder if staying healthy is possible. With life expectancy rising in the United States and in many other countries, we might question the state of our health if we should celebrate our 100th birthday! For an overview of personal health and what it might mean to stay healthy, let's look at four categories:

1. PHYSICAL HEALTH: When someone asks: "How are you today?", we assume our response depends on our state of physical health. We easily engage in conversations related to our physical well-being. Many of us have more than one doctor to keep us physically fit (primary care physician, dentist, optometrist, audiologist, dermatologist, cardiologist, and so on). Given the cost of medical care, health insurance is a major necessity. Because we highly value our physical health, we get the doctor's prescriptions filled quickly and pay whatever the cost. We are also told to pay attention to healthy eating and regular exercise. For those older adults who are motivated to push themselves beyond perceived age limits, amazing things can happen. For instance: my college-days buddy who wins international competition in the pole-vault event at age 88; fellow resident at my retirement community who competes nationally in golf tournaments at age 95; a former college professor who at age 100 leads physical exercises; the 103-year-old woman who at the National Senior Games ran the 50-meter dash in slightly over 20 seconds.

Granted not all of us "retirees" have the physical aptitude, discipline, and determination as those who make the newspaper headlines, yet individually we can do whatever it takes to maintain our physical health. One size does not fit all, but all of us can stay as healthy as possible within the constantly changing limitations of the aging process. On a retreat I met Frank Cunningham, former editor and publisher of Ave Maria Press. In his book *Vesper Time: The Spiritual Practice of Growing Older*, he has a good word for all of us, regardless of our state of health. "I find hope and inspiration in the courage of others who at Vesper Time (their later years) stand up to suffering and diminishment, accept its reality without crumbling into whiny self-pity."[40] And, for those readers whose primary physical workout is walking, I share Cunningham's regimen: Every day walk as far as you can, as fast as you can, for as long as you can.

2. MENTAL AND EMOTIONAL HEALTH: When my friend Jim Tarr, former CEO of Boy Scouts of America, was diagnosed with a prostate malignancy, he sent me a message requesting prayer and enclosed this positive thought.

CANCER IS LIMITED

It cannot cripple love...It cannot shatter hope...It cannot corrode faith.

It cannot destroy peace...It cannot kill friendship...It cannot suppress memories.

It cannot silence courage...It cannot invade the soul...It cannot conquer the spirit.

It cannot steal eternal life.

Jim Tarr lived on for several years, thanks to his positive attitude, medical treatments, and Christian faith. We know that the mind has tremendous influence over the body. This poster I saw one day proclaims a lesson for all of us.

ATTITUDE IS THE PAINTBRUSH OF THE MIND.
IT CAN COLOR ANY SITUATION.

Perhaps you know someone who is discouraged and feeling hopeless. Could you be an encourager with a listening ear? A registered nurse told me one day, "When I distribute medicine each day to the patients on my hospital wing, I try to give them hope along with their pills."

I think about the vast numbers of people who listen and watch the news on TV, the last thing before going to bed at night and the first thing when they wake up in the morning. With all the tragedies, terrorism, natural disasters, and criminal activities being reported every day, their minds are filled with the bad-news-oriented world. A spiritual and effective antidote is attendance at church worship services to hear some good news and to get a positive perspective on life. I find worship to be very therapeutic in maintaining mental health. Pause a moment to reflect on Paul's Letter to the Romans 12:2 CEB. "Don't be conformed to the patterns of this world, but be transformed by the renewing of your minds so that you can figure out what God's will is, what is good and pleasing and mature."

Related to our mental health is emotional or inner healing, sometimes called the healing of memories. Many of us have memories of abusive people, traumatic events, and hurtful situations that continue to cause us pain and discomfort. A therapy for inner healing, from a Christian perspective, is to invite the Healing Christ to go back to those painful memories in our past, to heal the hurt, and to bring release from bondage to those negative memories. Flora Wuellner's book *Prayer, Stress, & Our Inner Wounds* is an excellent resource that I highly recommend.[41]

3. HEALTHY RELATIONSHIPS: When we analyze the healing ministry of Jesus, the Gospel records show us his compassion and concern for people who had troubled or unhealthy relationships. Jesus definitely engaged in counseling ministry. His conversation with the Samaritan woman at the well hones in on her several unhealthy relationships (John 4:5-29).

As a pastor I discovered that healing personal relationships is often much more complicated and difficult than healing physical illnesses. The most effective therapy in healing human relationships is forgiveness. In Chapter 12 we will discuss the many facets and facts of forgiveness.

4. SPIRITUAL HEALTH: Our relationship with God is the heart of our spiritual health. Paul Tournier, the famous Swiss physician, believed that a spiritual unrest underlies almost every chronic and acute illness. Another medical doctor has stated that 25 percent of his patients could be cured by medical means alone, but that 75 percent needed the best medical care and the best spiritual care combined. Increasingly, medical science is seeing the value of the spiritual component in the healing process. Practicing physician Dale A. Matthews is a credible voice for what he calls "the faith factor." Based on research data we now have, Dr. Matthews is convinced that doctors (strictly from a scientific point of view) could recommend to their patients religious involvement in faith communities to improve their chances of being able to:

- stay healthy and avoid life-threatening and disabling diseases like cancer and heart disease;
- recover faster and with fewer complications if they do develop a serious illness; live longer;
- encounter terminal illnesses with greater peacefulness and less pain;
- avoid mental illnesses like depression and anxiety; cope more effectively with stress;
- steer clear of problems with alcohol, drugs, tobacco;
- enjoy a happier marriage and family life;
- find a greater sense of meaning and purpose in life.[42]

When ministering with the Navajo tribe in Arizona, I learned that should a Navajo get sick, the first act is to pray to the Great Spirit for help and healing. Then if relief is still needed, make an appointment with a medical doctor. Those of us who are not Native American usually reverse this pattern when we are ill. First we go to the doctor for diagnosis and medical care. Then if that does not work, we turn to God in prayer.

Several years ago on a Saturday morning in a Louisville, Kentucky, hospital, I was conducting a workshop (from a Christian point of view) on the significance of prayer in the healing process. About halfway into my presentation, a man raised his hand for attention. He identified himself as a Jewish physician and said, "I just want to say that Christians do not have a monopoly on healing." This was followed by several moments of absolute silence as everyone waited for my response. "You are correct, Doctor," I said. "Our Creator God has many, many ways to heal us. Christians do not have a monopoly on healing, but they believe in and follow Christ, who had a very active healing ministry. My role is to encourage Christians to have the best medical care and to pray, calling on the healing Christ when they are sick."

I have categorized four different kinds of health. This approach is helpful for clarity and discussion; however, in actuality these various health experiences overlap and need to be viewed in a holistic way. This definition or description of health is well stated:

"Health is a combination of harmonious relationships, spiritual vitality, psychological maturity, and physical wellness."[43]

I have never met a human being who is 100 percent healthy in all four categories at the same time (including myself). This is especially true with older adults, who even when their physical health declines can still enjoy spiritual health, mental health, and healthy relationships. When asked why I encourage myself and others to work at staying healthy as long as possible, two scriptures come to mind. "Don't you know that your body is a temple of the Holy Spirit who is in you?" (1 Corinthians 6:19 CEB). I do believe that is true; therefore, I desire to give God maximum mileage with my physical being as long as I live.

Then, this positive, hope-filled word:

"So we do not lose heart. Even though our outer nature is wasting away, our inner nature is being renewed day by day. For this slight momentary affliction is preparing us for an eternal weight of glory beyond all measure, because we look not at what can be seen but at what cannot be seen; for what can be seen is temporary, but what cannot be seen is eternal" (2 Corinthians 4:16-18 NRSV).

Let it be said as clearly as possible, that our loving, caring, gracious Creator God does not impose sickness, disease, and accidents to punish or to teach us a lesson. God is on the side of health, healing, and abundant life. Yet, there are those even in our churches who feel or believe that God causes unhealthiness. True story: In my first pastoral appointment there was a dear, sweet older lady who fell at home on a Sunday morning and broke a leg. When I visited her in the hospital she said, "Oh, Pastor, if I had come to church last Sunday morning and not stayed home, I would not have fallen and landed in the hospital. I think God was trying to tell me something." Several months after that episode, this same woman, on a Sunday morning, broke a leg in the church parking lot. No doubt she had to change her theology and not blame God for her tendency to fall.

When healing does not happen, those times when pain and suffering consume our attention, unanswerable questions arise, asking: "Where is God in all of this?" In the 1950s Methodist Minister Albert E. Day was the pastor of a church in Baltimore, MD, where he offered Services of Prayer and Healing once a week. In his book *Letters on the Healing Ministry,* first published in 1964, Pastor Day shares his experiences in helping people understand holistic health (physical, mental, spiritual).

"I must confess that the times when God has seemed most near and

God's grace most blessed have not always been when someone was healed of sickness, but in the hours when there was no physical healing but rather a healing of the spirit. Then came a glory that transcended all our hopes, and an assurance that death itself could not dilute or destroy...Of this much we are certain: for some whom we pray will experience a physical healing which could not otherwise have been their happy lot; others will enter into a blessed, conscious comradeship with God; ...but all will know that the church and its ministers deeply care for them, feel their pains, share their griefs. The church will become a fellowship of those who bear the mark of pain, which is, strangely enough, a fellowship of unique joy.[44]

Consider these affirmations of God's healthy intentions:

God's creation of the earth as described in Genesis 1:31, "God saw everything he had made and it was supremely good." One of our astronauts in viewing Earth from outer space declared, "It looks like a garden planet."

The natural ability of the human body to heal itself. Doctors do not heal us. Their role is to prescribe whatever will work with the body's healing capabilities. Dr. Albert Schweitzer once remarked, "I just try to connect with the doctor inside of you."

The research, discoveries, resources of the medical profession.

The intentional and effective healing ministry of Jesus Christ. He never told sick people that God was teaching them a lesson or that God's will was for them to be unhealthy.

In closing I offer you this paraphrase of St. Francis' prayer. You may want to pray this for yourself or others when coping with unhealthiness:

Gracious, loving, caring God, source of life, health, and wholeness,

Make me be an instrument of your healing grace.

When I am weak and in pain, help me to rest in your love.

When I am anxious and worried, help me to wait patiently.

When I am afraid, help me to trust in you.

When I am lonely, help me to sense your presence.

Compassionate and healing God, help me not to demand everything from myself, but to allow others to help me.

Grant me not so much to escape life's uncertainties, but to face situations and learn the depths of your caring love.

For it is in being uncertain and not in control that I find true faith.

In knowing the limits of my mind and body that I find wholeness and health of my spirit.

In passing through death that I find life that lasts forever.

In the name of Jesus, the Christ, my Savior, Healer, and Lord,

I offer myself to you.   Amen.

QUESTIONS TO PONDER

1. What are some helpful, practical things you do to stay healthy?

2. How do you respond to these two scripture verses noted in this chapter? 1 Corinthians 6:19 and 2 Corinthians 4:16-18

3. What limitations are you presently experiencing: physically, mentally, spiritually, or in relationships? Take a sheet of paper and make a list of these in a column on the left side. Then make a column on the right side of the paper listing good things in your life that seem to compensate for your diminishments.

4. As we get older we tend to take more and more pills. . Do you ever pause to thank God for your medicines, for the doctors who prescribed them, and for theresearchers who discovered and developed health-enhancing therapies?

Chapter 9

TWIN VIRTUES: COMPASSION
& ENCOURAGEMENT

*"The Lord is good to all, and His compassion
is over all that He has made."*
(Psalm 145:9 NRSV)

Questions: When I get discouraged and full of negative thoughts, I wonder if anyone else feels this way? Is anyone out there who can help me?

Reflection: Compassion and encouragement go together, live together, are experienced together, and cannot be separated. Compassion leads to encouragement. Are all of us compassionate encouragers? At times we are; but we can also be inconsistent and hesitant when it comes to leaving our comfort zone to assist those in need. Whereas, children seem to have natural feelings and desires to be helpful. I think of young girls and boys who bring home stray cats and dogs without permission. Or, take this story about the little girl who was late coming home from school one afternoon. Her mother, being both worried and annoyed, demanded an explanation.

"Mommy," said her daughter, "I was just walking home with my friend Julie and halfway here Julie dropped her favorite doll and it broke into lots of little pieces."

"Oh, honey," replied the mother, "so you were late because you helped Julie pick up the pieces to put her doll back together."

But then, in her young and innocent voice, the little girl said, "No, Mommy, I didn't know how to fix the doll. I just stayed with Julie to help her cry."

Have you noticed that in times of national emergencies (bombing of Pearl Harbor that launched WWII on December 7, 1941; the terrorist attacks in the United States on September 11, 2001; the COVID-19 coronavirus pandemic in 2020), humanitarian assistance springs up immediately and automatically with strangers and neighbors rising to the moment. Likewise when horrific natural disasters strike (tornadoes, hurricanes, floods, forest fires, earthquakes), we witness widespread compassion in action. But then, when life settles in and stability returns, we tend to reserve our caring attitudes, actions, and generosity for those who are more like us or for those who belong to our club or go to our school or live in our neighborhood.

Compassion and encouragement are necessities for humanity the world over. Their significance and importance are not the teachings and practices of any one religion, but are basic components of many spiritual traditions. Perhaps you will be impressed as I am with this true story about the exiled spiritual leader of the Tibetan people, the Dalai Lama. In his book *The Art of Happiness* is his speech to a standing-room-only audience at Arizona State University in 1993. These are his opening words:

"I think that this is the first time I am meeting most of you. But to me, whether it is an old friend or a new friend, there's not much difference anyway, because I always believe we are the same; we are all human beings. Of course, there may be differences in cultural background or way of life, there may be differences in our faith, or we may be of a different color, but we are human beings, consisting of the human body and the human mind. Our physical structure is the same, and our mind and our emotional nature are also the same. Wherever I meet people, I always have the feeling that I am encountering another human being just like myself. I find it is much easier to communicate with others on that level. If you want others to be happy practice compassion; and if you want to be happy practice compassion...a state of mind that is non-violent, non-harming, and non-aggressive. Compassion is a mental attitude based on the wish for others to be free of their suffering and is associated with a sense of commitment, responsibility, and respect towards the other."[45]

Compassion and encouragement are significant virtues that can be practiced by everyone: secular humanists, atheists, agnostics, the nones (those who claim no religious affiliation), as well as those who adhere to and practice various religions of the world. Here is a closer look at these commendable qualities of life.

ENCOURAGEMENT: Legend has it that one time the devil was planning to locate in another part of the world and decided to have a "relocation sale." Many tools of his trade that could be replaced later were now on sale. In came a potential customer and noticed that one item in particular had the most expensive price tag. "Why," he asked the devil, "are you asking so much money for your tool of discouragement?" "Think about it," responded the devil, "with discouragement I can easily pry into people's lives and offer them a ton of temptations."

So true, is it not? When you and I become discouraged for whatever reason or circumstance, life can easily go downhill from there. When I recall my personal times of being discouraged, it was an encouraging word from a friend, a teacher, a family member, or a verse in the Bible that stopped the skid downward. Sometimes the encouragement was not in words, but in a kind act or a gift, a listening ear, a hug with a smile. Think about your own days of discouragement. Who or what entered your life and made a helpful difference when you most needed it?

Encouraging others is not complicated. Could be a handwritten note, a "thinking about you" card in the mail, a phone call, text, or email message. Dr. Richard Gunderman, who teaches medical students at Indiana University, calls the benefits of well-wishers "The Trebek Effect," named after Alex Trebek, the long-time host of TV's *Jeopardy* game show, who reported in May 2019 that his stage four pancreatic cancer was in near remission. He went on to thank hundreds of thousands of people who reached out to him with personal communications. Dr. Gunderman, who is especially sensitive to hospitalized patients, went on to say, "Just our presence can make a big difference. We need to recognize how powerful that can be. Every one of us can reach out to somebody who's lonely and discouraged." The Rev. Jim Zappy, corporate chaplain for National Church Residences that offers senior housing and services, knows firsthand the healing effect of encouragement, stating, "Isolation has an impact on us physically and emotionally. What happens to me emotionally impacts me physically."[46]

The Apostle Paul, whose letters to fledgling churches in the first century comprise more than half of the Christian scriptures, soon after his conversion recruited a traveling companion whose name speaks volumes. They called him Barnabas, which means "son of encouragement" (Acts 4:36). Paul was also an encourager. He wrote to one congregation, "Encourage one another and build up one another" (I Thess. 5:11 CEB). Everyone (follower or leader) needs encouragement. No doubt this is why Jesus, early in his public ministry, invited twelve men to be his inner circle of companions. This excellent statement by John Maxwell reminds all of us to be encouragers when encouragement is needed: "To encourage people is to help them gain courage they might not otherwise possess, courage to face the day, to do what is right, to take risks, to make a difference. The heart of encouragement is to communicate a person's value."[47]

COMPASSION: The word "compassion" is from the Latin "com," meaning "with," and "passio" for "suffering or distress." Literally the Latin means: to feel the distress of another person in your gut with a desire to give assistance. Genuine compassion begins with an uncomfortable feeling deep within us. This empathetic feeling leads to a desire to do something helpful. This desire, then, initiates benevolent action. A classic example of compassionate action in the Bible is the parable Jesus told about a man who was beat up, robbed, and left half dead in a roadside ditch. Two passersby saw the injured man and felt sorry (sympathy) for him but went on their way. Another passerby, when he saw the helpless victim, experienced an uncomfortable feeling (empathy) that led to stopping and offering assistance. Then came beneficial action. As Jesus told this story: "But a Samaritan came to where the victim was; and when he saw him, he was moved with compassion, went to him and bound up his wounds, pouring on oil and wine (first aid). Then he set the man on his donkey and brought him to an inn." Giving the innkeeper a money-advance, he said, "Take care of him; and what ever more you spend, I will repay you when I come back"(Luke 10:29-37 CEB).

Compassion is related to sympathy, kindness, mercy, pity, and empathy; however, it is more than a passing emotion or a polite courtesy. Opportunities abound for being a compassionate human being. Offering a word of encouragement is an act of compassion. Intercessory prayer (praying for others) certainly comes under the caring umbrella of compassion. In the retirement community where I live, I witness acts of compassion, not only by the staff, but also among the residents.

- Off-campus day trips would not be possible for residents who are physically challenged getting on and off the bus without the helping hands of other residents.
- I heard of a resident getting up in the middle of the night to drive another resident to the hospital ER.
- When a resident dies, close friends take turns sitting and grieving together.
- Then there are the veteran residents who take personal interests in rookie residents that go well beyond the initial orientation period.
- Recently I learned of a resident who sat by a terminally ill resident (who had no family) holding hands during his final hours.

Granted, for some of us being a compassionate person comes naturally and without hesitation. For others (even the crusty, critical, grumbling curmudgeons among us), it is possible to develop a caring attitude and to move out of our comfort zones when situations and circumstances beg for our attention.

Before offering encouragement and compassion, I pause to pray, asking our loving, caring God for personal guidance and for blessings on everyone in the circle of concern.

When reviewing The Ten Commandments (Exodus 20:1-17), I notice there is no mandate: "Thou shalt be an encouraging, compassionate human being." However, I have learned that all of the major world religions teach a version of the Golden Rule: "Treat people in the same way that you want people to treat you" (Matthew 7:12 CEB). The Bible contains many teachings on compassion and encouragement. Jesus is the role model exemplar in living out these twin virtues. He expected his followers to do likewise. As he taught: "Love your neighbor as yourself" (Mark 12:31 CEB). My neighbor is anyone in need. As the Apostle Paul wrote: "Carry each other's burdens and so you will fulfill the law of Christ" (Galatians 6:2 CEB).

QUESTIONS TO PONDER

1. Name some of the times you were discouraged. Can you recall who or what came to your assistance?

2. Name some of the people to whom you reached out. What word of encouragement or act of compassion did you offer?

3. What are some things you could do to develop a lifestyle of being compassionate and encouraging to others?

4. Consider this statement by Flora Edwards: "In helping others, we shall help ourselves, for whatever good we give out completes the circle and comes back to us." Have you experienced this benevolent boomerang effect?[48]

Chapter 10

GRACE: GOD'S LOVE IN ACTION

*"Grace is the free undeserved goodness
and favor of God to humanity."*
—Matthew Henry

QUESTIONS: Why is it that the hymn "Amazing Grace" is so popular, even among those who have little or no church connection? And what is the relationship between God's love and God's grace?

REFLECTION: Year after year this hymn stays at the top of the most liked hymn-list. We hear it played and sung frequently, not only in church services, but also on bagpipes at memorial ceremonies, major public events, and national holidays. Could it be that the simple, haunting melody, combined with the plain, unadorned, poetic truth of the verses, communicates at a deep level touching the souls of the hearers? Let's take a closer look at some verses in the hymn "Amazing Grace."[49]

Verse 1, Amazing grace! How sweet the sound that saved a wretch like me! I once was lost but now am found; was blind, but now I see.

The words "a wretch" have caused some to say, "I do not consider myself a wretch. When I sing this hymn I change 'a wretch' to 'someone like me.'" However, when we acquaint ourselves with the background to this hymn, we may well conclude that "a wretch like me" is quite appropriate for the composer John Newton (1725–1807). Prior to being ordained in the Church of England, he served as a ship captain in the slave trade of his day. His conversion to Christianity opened his eyes to the evils of slavery ("I once was blind, but now I see"). In reflecting on his wretched early life, Newton believed it was solely the amazing, unexplainable grace of God that brought him to Christ. "How sweet the sound that saved…" Newton became a strong voice and advocate to abolish slavery, living to see England's abolition of the African slave trade in 1807, just before his death. Many who sing this hymn today do not stumble over the words "a wretch like me" when being honest with God. Likewise, with God's grace quietly working on our moral and ethical blindness, we too can experience spiritual insight and heartily sing "I once was blind, but now I see."

Verse 3, Through many dangers, toils, and snares, I have already come; 'tis grace hath brought me safe thus far and grace will lead me home.

Every time I sing this verse, it brings instant recall to episodes in my past of coming too close to real danger, demanding work, and tempting situations that tried to snare and drag me down. But the line ends on a note of assurance and hope, believing that God's grace protects me now and in the life to come, as stated in the next verse.

Verse 4, Yes, when this flesh and heart shall fail, and mortal life shall cease, I shall possess, within the veil, a life of joy and peace.

During your solitude and silence time, think about this amazing hymn, written over 200 years ago, and why or how it may connect with you. You can locate all of the verses in most hymn books or on the Internet.

Moving on, let's look at the definition of "grace." This often used word in the New Testament comes from the Greek "charis," which translates in English: benefit, favor, divine influence or gift. This is also the root of "charisma," which means gratuity, spiritual endowment, or gift. Interpretation: God's grace cannot be earned through human effort, good work, or pious behavior. When we begin to be mindful of the ever-present grace of God, we know we did nothing to deserve it; nor do we receive grace as a reward for any human endeavor. Awareness of God's grace in our lives can lead to spiritual awakening that may occur anywhere, at any time from childhood to old age.

It was the Apostle Paul's understanding and emphasis of God's grace that caught Martin Luther's attention in the 16th century. Luther's reading and interpretation of Paul's Letter to the Church at Ephesus sparked the Reformation of the Church. "For by grace you have been saved through faith, and this is not your own doing; it is the gift of God, not the result of works, so that no one may boast" (Ephesians 2:8-9 NRSV).

Given his history of persecuting Christians, Paul would have had no hesitation in singing "grace that saves a wretch like me." Paul must have been dazzled by the overwhelming nature of this newly discovered grace of God. Here is a clue to his usage of words like unsearchable, incomprehensible, unfathomable in describing God's grace. Recalling his spiritual journey, Paul wrote, "God gave his grace to me, the least of all God's people, to preach the good news about the immeasurable riches of Christ to the Gentiles" (Ephesians 3:8 CEB).

Paul's ministry was anything but easy. The obstacles, resistance, suffering, and pain he faced are beyond description. Yet he wrote these encouraging words he received from the Holy Spirit and are quoted by today's Christians: "My grace is sufficient for you" (2 Corinthians 12:9 NRSV).

As we continue to spotlight God's amazing grace, turn to the Gospel of John. In Chapter One is John's profound statement that the creating Word of God came to our planet in the form of a human baby. "The Word became flesh and made his home among us. We have seen his glory, glory like that of a father's only son full of grace and truth. From his fullness we have all received grace upon grace" (John 1:14,16 CEB).

What could be the meaning and intent of the phrase "grace upon grace"? Each day, each month, each year our personal situations are constantly changing. "Grace upon grace" could be John's way of expressing the limitlessness of the Word incarnate in Jesus, who, full of grace and truth, rose from the grave and, as the Risen Christ, extravagantly and faithfully shares God's grace each day to help us cope with our everyday situations. As we sing: "Great is thy faithfulness! Morning by morning new mercies I see; all I have needed thy hand hath provided; great is thy faithfulness, Lord, unto me!"[50] Because God's grace is never exhausted, is present and willing to bless us each day, whatever the day may bring forth, we gladly sing, "Amazing grace, how sweet the sound." Sweeter still is the reality and experience of God's grace.

What is the relationship between God's love and God's grace? The short answer is in the title of this chapter: Grace is God's love in action. God's love is the foundation, the motivation, the genesis of God's grace. Yes, love and grace go together, but love is the catalyst and heartbeat of grace. Here is a small sampling of the primacy of God's love as recorded in the New Testament.

"God so loved the world that God gave his only Son" (John 3:16 RSV).

"A new commandment I give you that you love one another as I have loved you," Jesus to the Apostles (John 13:34 RSV).

"Dear friends, let us love one another because love is from God, and everyone who loves is born from God, because God is love" (I John 4:7-8 CEB).

Contemplate John Mogabgab's wisdom: "In the mystery of divine love that Jesus embodies, there is at once no distance and yet immeasurable spaciousness between God and humanity. God's love seeks the most profound intimacy with us, but never in ways that encroach on our freedom. Love is a constant commitment lived gently, compassionately, intelligently. Love draws out what is truest and best in whatever it touches. Love guides and shapes all toward wholeness. Love is quietly victorious."[51]

So how does one describe or define this all-encompassing love of God? Paul wrote:

"Faith, hope, and love remain, these three things, and the greatest of these is love" (I Corinthians 13:13 CEB).

Now go back to the beginning of this "love chapter." In the contemporary translation of Eugene H. Peterson in The Message (I Corinthians 13:1-3):

> If I speak with human eloquence and angelic ecstasy but don't love, I'm nothing but the creaking of a rusty gate. If I speak God's word with power, revealing all his mysteries and making everything plain as day, and if I have faith that says to

a mountain "Jump" and it jumps, but I don't love, I'm nothing. If I give away everything I own to the poor and even go to the stake to be burned as a martyr, but I don't love, I've gotten nowhere. So, no matter what I say, what I believe, and what I do, I'm bankrupt without love.

Paul then proceeds to give sixteen traits or characteristics of God's love. Each line begins with the word "Love." Right now I encourage you to do a two-part exercise. First, as you read the next verses put the word Christ in the blank in front of each line. Why? Because here is a composite snapshot of Christ's values and lifestyle (I Corinthians 13:4-8).

_____ never gives up.

_____ cares more for others than for self.

_____ doesn't want what it doesn't have.

_____ doesn't strut.

_____ doesn't have a swelled head

_____ doesn't force itself on others.

_____ isn't always "me first."

_____ doesn't fly off the handle.

_____ doesn't keep score of the sins of others.

_____ doesn't revel when others grovel.

_____ takes pleasure in the flowering of truth.

_____ trusts God always.

_____ always looks for the best.

_____ never looks back.

_____ keeps going to the end.

_____ never dies.

For the second part of this exercise, reread these verses and this time insert your name in the blank in front of each line. Why? Because you will quickly discern your present state of spiritual health, recognizing those areas of your life that seem to be on track and those that could use improvement. While each one of us has room for personal growth, "the great thing about God's love is that it is not determined by the object of God's love. God does not love us because we are good. God loves us because God is good."[52] Since we are created in the image of our Creator (Genesis 1:27), we are embedded with the love DNA and are expected to love God and other human beings. Some years ago I visited a church in Decatur, Illinois, and noticed on their letterhead this motto:

> OUR ROLE IS TO LOVE PEOPLE.
> GOD'S ROLE IS TO CHANGE PEOPLE.
> LET'S NOT CONFUSE THE TWO ROLES.

This reminded me of something I heard Rev. Morton Kelsey say in a sermon, "The sign of health in my spiritual life is how much love is flowing through me." Notice he did not say how much love am I receiving and keeping for myself. So ask yourself this question: "How much love is flowing through me this moment, this day, reaching out to other people?" Our loving God desires for each of us to love and to be loved. When we are on the receiving end, we are experiencing God's amazing grace, and when we are on the giving end, we are sharing God's grace with other people. Grace is God's love in action.

QUESTIONS TO PONDER

1. Some of us still cling to the notion that we have to earn "good points" in order to be worthy of God's love and grace. How does that thinking compare to the following statement? God does not love us because we are good. God loves us because God is good.

2. Can you think of some amazing grace moments in your life? If so, write them down, and be thankful and alert to future grace-filled blessings.

3. Granted, it is not easy to love everyone, especially those who are difficult and hard to get along with. What are some ways you could share God's grace with people like that?

4. What does this bit of prose by John Newton say to you?

    I am not what I ought to be.
    I am not what I want to be
    I am not what I hope to be.
    I am not what I used to be.
    And by the grace of God I am what I am.[53]

Chapter 11

GRATITUDE AND APPRECIATION

"Gratitude is the mother of all other virtues."

—Cicero

Question: When I was younger it seemed easier to be thankful than it is now. Does gratitude diminish with old age?

Reflection: A friend of mine had a life-changing experience while browsing at a farmers market. Here is his telling of the true story: My wife and I were shopping one summer morning at our local farmers market, admiring the beautiful produce. As we leisurely walked along we came upon a stall selling sweet corn. I had to stop, read, and re-read the sign:

FREE SWEET CORN — FREE SWEET CORN

Said I to the vendor, "Is that sign for real?"

"Certainly is. If you want to take me up on my offer you can have a dozen ears free to take home."

"Okay, tell me more."

"You buy one dozen and I'll throw in an extra dozen, if you promise me that when you get home you will give away the free corn to someone who needs it more than you do."

"Well sure," I said, "that's a deal." Then I paid him for one dozen.

When we returned home we had a lengthy discussion about giving away the sweet corn. We knew several families who would be glad to have the corn. After delivering the dozen ears, I got to thinking, "Every summer I have this vegetable garden in the backyard that produces more than our family can ever eat, especially tomatoes. Maybe I could be like that farmer and give away my abundance to anyone in need." That was several summers ago. What a blessing this has been for the receivers and the givers. I am so thankful for that sweet corn farmer who changed my attitude on what it means to be a more grateful, generous human being.

Gratitude does not have to diminish as we get older as long as we do not get stuck in the past. As Frank Cunningham said it so well, "Gratitude is the antidote to the increasing constrictions of old age."[54] Or, to say that slightly differently, here is wisdom from the pen of Joan Rivers (comedienne/author): "Yesterday is history; tomorrow is a mystery; today is God's gift. That's why we call it the present."[55] We can be grateful for the presents (small and large) that come to us with the gift of each new day.

The key word and the operative experience in this chapter is "gratitude." From the Latin "gratus" comes several English words: gratitude, grateful, gratis, gratuity, gratuitous, and gratify. All of these express appreciation and thankfulness for benefits, blessings, helpfulness in life. Notice within the word "gratitude" is another significant word. If we add the letter "t" we have "attitude." A grateful attitude can become a positive lens through which we view our world and all the people around us. Take a quick self-check: Do I have a gratitude attitude? Or, does ingratitude tend to dominate my feelings and actions?

Given the daily media outpouring of "bad news," maintaining a positive outlook on life is not so easy. But we do have a choice, as stated so well by the great humanitarian Dr. Albert Schweitzer:

"We must take care not to adopt as part of a theory of life people's bitter sayings about the ingratitude of the world. A great deal of water is flowing underground which never comes up as a spring. In that thought we find comfort. But we ourselves must try to be the water which does find its way up; we must become a spring at which all can quench their thirst for gratitude."[56]

The realities of aging (cumulative health issues, everyday aches and pains, financial anxieties, and not being savvy in using smartphones, computers, iPads, tablets, Facebook, and emails) can feed a negative mindset. Some days we may find it easier to be a grumpy, grumbling, critical curmudgeon. However, in comparison to the curmudgeons of the world, "grateful people feel better emotionally, get sick less often, experience less stress brought on by depression and anxiety, take better care of themselves, and even sleep better."[57] Medical researchers are adding new insights to the positive relationship between gratitude and good health. Canadian Dr. Hans Selye, a biochemist, discovered that positive emotions (gratitude, thanksgiving, praise, and joy) are health-enhancing factors. Conversely, negative emotions have a debilitating and disease-inducing effect on the mind and body.[58]

So where does gratitude originate? What motivates a generous heart? What might be the causes of benevolent actions toward others? Actually there are several answers to these questions:

- response to the outpouring of God's grace and love;
- feelings of empathy or identification with the plight of others;
- being impressed with the generosity of people helping people;
- following the example of respected role models;
- simply sharing out of thankfulness for one's blessings.

Here are some real-life stories. Can you figure out what motivated these people to take benevolent actions?

LITTER-PICKER-UPPER: In our neighborhood is an older woman who consistently picks up the litter for several blocks while walking her dog each day.

FLOWER BED WEEDERS: In my retirement community we have two residents, one in her early 80s who uses a walker and one in her late 80s who uses a cane. In the spring and summer months they can be seen ignoring their physical limitations and weeding the flower beds. They are not on the Landscaping Committee and no one asked them to pull weeds.

PAYING FORWARD: In December one year I received in the mail a Walmart gift card for $100 with a note from a friend asking me to give this to a "needy family" in the church I was attending. Immediately I phoned my pastor with this generous offer and told her I would pass it on and she could give it to a needy family. "Oh," she responded, "that's great. I'll get back to you." Soon I received an email from her with the names of three families, asking me to select one to receive the $100. As I read over her message I decided that since I did not personally know any of them, I would donate another $100 Walmart gift card and that way two out of three families would be assisted. I sent her an email with this even more generous offer. Couple hours later, she sent me another message stating that after discussing the matter with her husband, they decided to add another $100 Walmart gift card. That way all three families would get unexpected pre-Christmas gifts.

Closely related to "gratitude" is "appreciation," a beautiful word loaded with positive uses and understandings. A close friend and fishing buddy of mine had a wonderful way of signing his notes, letters, and emails to me. He always ended with "You are appreciated." Appreciation is an expression of admiration, approval, or gratitude. When you tell someone that you appreciate them, you are saying they are valued and have much to offer as a unique human being. A book on this topic that I highly recommend is *The Power of Appreciation* by Adrian van Kaam and Susan Muto. Their opening paragraph reads: "Appreciation is the single most important disposition (prevailing tendency) to be cultivated in our life and world today. The power of appreciation helps us to look at the directions for living offered by everyday events, good and bad, and indifferent, in a new way."[59] When you express appreciation to someone, you are saying that you care about them. The best way to become an appreciative person is to be thankful to other people and especially to God from whom all blessings flow.

This leads us to some other words in the gratitude galaxy such as: thanks, thankful, thanksgiving. In the Hebrew Scriptures (OT) many of the Psalms express thankfulness to God, literally meaning "show open hands, to give, express praise" (See Psalm 92:1). Then there is this all-encompassing instruction from Paul in I Thessalonians 5:18 (NRSV), "Give thanks in all circumstances." Notice he does not say: Give thanks FOR all circumstances. Rather, express trust in God to bring something good out of the most trying and difficult situations, even when the silver lining is nowhere in sight.

Too often we forget that words can hurt or heal, hinder or help.

Offering the common courtesy of saying "thank you" never goes out of style. A Chinese proverb says: "A single kind word keeps one warm for three winters." Perhaps you can identify with this woman who wrote to columnist Ann Landers asking her to print "My Everyday Thanksgivings" and signed, Fan in Tampa, FL.

"Even though I clutch my blanket and growl when the alarm rings each morning, thank you, Lord, that I can hear. There are those who are deaf.

Even though I keep my eyes tightly closed against the morning light as long as possible, thank you, Lord, that I can see. There are many who are blind.

Even though I huddle in my bed and put off the effort of rising, thank you, Lord, that I have the strength to rise. There are many who are bedridden.

Even though my breakfast table never looks like the pictures in the magazines, and the menu is unbalanced, thank you, Lord, for my food, for there are many who are hungry.

Even though I grumble and complain and wish my circumstances were better, thank you, Lord, for the gift of life."[60]

Many of us growing up were encouraged to be generous and thankful. We may have been taught: "It is more blessed to give than to receive" (Acts 20:35 NRSV). One year when Christmas came on Sunday, I decided to do a dialogue sermon with the congregation in the morning worship service. My introduction went something like this:

"Christmas is a special time of giving and receiving gifts. I want each one of you to think about your gifts, not the ones you received, but the ones you gave to others. (Pause) Now in your mind,

of all the gifts you gave, select one that warmed your heart and filled you with joy." (Pause) Then I stepped away from the pulpit, with microphone in hand, walked among the congregation. "Would anyone like to tell us about one of the gifts you gave and how the receiver responded?" At that point, several hands went up and the most joyous sharing proceeded (much longer than a normal sermon). It was an unforgettable experience, an inter-generational happening, laughter and tears mixed with joy, gratitude, and appreciation. A true Christmas experience! That delightful time of sharing proved that giving and gratitude bless the receiver and the giver.

In this chapter I am highlighting gratitude, appreciation, and thankfulness to encourage all readers not only to value these essentials for healthy living and relationships, but also to be more mindful in practicing them. You might want to try these exercises or create your own.

- GRATITUDE JOURNAL: By your bedside keep a notepad and pen to record before you go to sleep at least five good things, helpful experiences, pleasant surprises that came your way that day.
- TEACHERS/ROLE MODELS/MENTORS: Make a list of all the persons in your life who had and continue to have a positive influence. Name any and all who expanded your world, opened up possibilities and opportunities for which you are truly grateful. Bless each one in thanksgiving to God.
- ALPHABET THANK LIST: On a blank paper jot down the 26 letters of the English alphabet in a column on the left-hand side. Then beside each letter write someone or something that begins with that letter for which you are thankful.
- COUNTING SHEEP: Before dropping off to sleep each night,

rather than counting sheep, speak with the Good Shepherd about whatever is on your heart and mind. Or, as the hymn goes: "Count your many blessings, name them one by one, and it will surprise you what the Lord has done."

QUESTIONS TO PONDER

1. Have you had any experiences similar to the FREE SWEET CORN story?

2. What personally motivates you to express gratitude and appreciation?

3. When someone says to you "thank you," how does that feel? Have you ever said to another person, "You are appreciated"? Or, has anyone ever expressed their appreciation for you?

4. From your personal life experiences what could you add to these thanksgiving thoughts by Joseph Andrew Halatek (written in 1987)?

    > Closer comes the moment
    > When all are thankful for
    > The many blessings of the past
    > And the ones that lay in store.
    >
    > Thankful are the many hearts
    > Upon Thanksgiving Day
    > When everyone seems thankful,
    > And some will even pray.
    >
    > Why is it, then, that we must wait
    > Upon occasions special
    > To give thanks for all life's blessings
    > When each day it is essential?

Oft' are the times we run about
While never giving thought
To daily blessings we possess
And some we've never sought.

Our lives are much too busy
As these blessings come and go;
We pass them off so frivolous
Our thankful hearts don't show.

A solution to this problem
Is to open up our mind
And start each day by looking
For the blessings we may find.

Then, every day is special
With thanksgiving on our heart
And, blessings abound forever.
Never to depart.[61]

Chapter 12

FORGIVENESS: A GIFT TO GIVE AND RECEIVE

Forgiveness: To stop feeling angry or resentful towards someone for an offense, flaw, or mistake.
The New Oxford Dictionary

QUESTION: Why is it so difficult to forgive those who hurt you?

REFLECTION:

Before we discuss this common human dilemma, consider another story told about those legendary figures the Lone Ranger and Tonto. Out on the open prairie, they pitched their tent and went to bed. In the middle of the night Tonto woke up and decided to awaken his companion.

Tonto: "Lone Ranger, wake up…wake up and tell me what you see."

Looking up, the Lone Ranger says: "Well, Tonto, I see millions of stars."

Tonto: "And what do you think it means to look up and see millions of stars?"

After giving this question some thought, the Lone Ranger said, "Astrologically it means there are solar systems and galaxies that hold all of those stars together. Theologically it means that God is all-powerful and amazing in creating all of that. It also tells me that given the placement of the moon, time-wise, it is about 3:30 in the morning. And, meteorologically speaking, it tells me that tomorrow is going to be a beautiful day. What do all those stars mean to you, Tonto?"

Tonto replies: "Lone Ranger, it means to me that you are dumb as a buffalo. Someone has stolen our tent."

When we, for any reason, withhold forgiveness or refuse to accept forgiveness, we too are dumb as a buffalo. Why is that? It's called the boomerang effect. You might think you are doing someone a favor by forgiving them. The truth is that forgiveness returns to bless the giver more times than it blesses the intended receiver. The boomerang effect is also operative when forgiveness is not offered, causing a negative impact on the unforgiving person.

As we unpack this complicated topic and look more closely at its many facets and facts, ponder the following:

I am highly sought after, but strangely elusive.

I am taught faithfully to children, but rarely lived by the tutors.

I am romanticized in poems and novels, but seldom seen in everyday life.

I am first cousin to mercy and love, but all too absent in the human family.

I am related to forgetting, but not kin to amnesia.

I am a key to good health, but hardly used to unlock benefits unlimited.

I am an antidote for dealing with stress-filled relationships, but kept hidden in resentful hearts.

I am the topic of many sermons, but living examples are hard to come by.

I am not impossible, but am perceived to be improbable and impractical.

I am needed in many lives, but no one wants to go first.

I am a chance to start over, a sign of hope, and a therapeutic action that can cure this world's ills.

I am a gift from God for giving to others.

I am a gift from God for receiving from others.

I AM FORGIVENESS.

Returning to the question: Why is it so difficult to forgive those who hurt you? Answer: Because forgiveness and being a forgiving person are contrary to our basic human nature. This holds true for elderly adults, very young children, and every age in between. We are born into this world with an all-encompassing desire to protect ourselves whatever the cost. To illustrate, watch preschoolers at play. Observe how they instinctively hit back when someone hits them or tries to take a toy away from them. Forgiveness is a learned response and not automatically employed when needed. This means that every time you and I get hurt we have to make a conscious decision what to do next. Do we try to get even, harbor resentment, stay mad, or make an attempt to repair the relationship and move on with our life? We do have a choice.

Consider this partial list of misconceptions. Forgiveness is not…

- covering up the conflict.
- coexisting peacefully.
- making excuses for bad behavior.
- tolerating the situation.
- condoning unkindness and harmful actions.
- trying to forget.
- self-sacrificing.
- denying our hurts and feelings.
- being a long-suffering martyr.
- setting conditional limits.
- smiling no matter what happens.

If you have practiced any of the above, even with good intentions and in the name of forgiveness, then you have experienced limitations and discouragement. Lewis Smedes offers a more positive understanding of forgiveness. "Forgiveness is God's invention for coming to terms with a world in which, despite their best intentions, people are unfair to each other and hurt each other deeply. Forgiving is love's toughest work, and love's biggest risk. If you twist it into something it was never meant to be, it can make you a doormat or an insufferable manipulator. Forgiving seems almost unnatural. Our sense of fairness tells us people should pay for the wrong they do. But forgiving is love's power to break nature's rule."[62]

In recent years forgiveness-research has become a budding and growing science, attracting investigators who are motivated to explore the relationship between forgiveness and health. These scientific studies are affirming the healing power of forgiveness. Dr. Fred Luskin, a pioneer in this research and co-founder of the Stanford University Forgiveness Project, is convinced that "learning to forgive is good for both your mental and physical well-being, and your relationships."[63]

COMPARE THESE TWO COLUMNS FROM FORGIVENESS RESEARCH

Unforgiveness can release:	Forgiveness can bring:
Anger	Calm
Shame	Joy
Bitterness	Mercy
Guilt	Relief
Embarrassment	Delight
Revenge	Compassion
Depression	Peacefulness
Ingratitude	Thankfulness
Jealousy	Acceptance
Hate	Grace
Close-mindedness	Open-mindedness
Negative attitudes	Positive attitudes
Cursing	Blessing
Intolerance	Love
Hopelessness	Hope
Suspicion	Trust
Resentment	Appreciation
Bondage	Freedom

Several years ago, I discovered the teachings of Dr. Doris Donnelly, college professor and author, who promotes a very practical approach in the forgiveness process with this three-step format.[64]

Step One: I am hurt and upset by someone.

Step Two: I name the hurtful issue and choose to forgive.

Step Three: I attempt reconciliation.

Our basic human instinct is to not go beyond Step One. Simply lick our wounds, plot some ways to get even, or just stay upset and try to live with the hurtful issue. Moving from Step One to Step Two takes some time. How much time? Do not rush. Could take five minutes, five hours, five days, five weeks, five years or longer. Time does not heal, but time offers the needed space to deal with one's damaged feelings and identify what actually went wrong in the relationship. To move too quickly from Step One to Step Two is not helpful. To never move is worse. Step Two involves a conscious decision to not stay stuck with an unforgiving attitude and to choose to extend forgiveness to the other person. That is a big, big step forward. This prompts some questions: Yes, I choose to forgive, but how am I going to do it? What are some ways I can communicate forgiveness? Should I meet face-to-face? Or, maybe a phone call, email, Facebook, perhaps a hand-written letter? Then comes Step Three. Underline the words "attempt reconciliation." By definition reconciliation means to restore broken relationships, to come together in harmony and friendship, to have a mutual settlement of disagreements.

Reconciliation is a worthy goal, but not always achievable. It takes both persons to reconcile. If one party is not interested, that concludes the process. We need to make an attempt at reconciliation, but not beat up ourselves with guilt if it does not happen.

Another common aspect of forgiveness is forgiving and forgetting.

"Well, you have not really forgiven someone unless you forget everything. Forgive and forget is the goal," some people would say. My response is simply that amnesia is not part of the equation. We do not ask God to erase certain memories of our past. The forgiveness process is complete when we can recall the hurtful person or the damaging event without remembering or re-feeling the pain, the injury, and the distress associated with that incident. The goal is to forgive the person and let go of the pain. But do not forget the damaging circumstances or you may repeat the experience in the future.

When should one initiate the healing process? When one's emotions are ready, when more positive feelings begin to surface? No. If we wait until we feel like forgiving someone we may never get around to doing it. Forgiveness begins with a decision of the mind, not the emotions of the heart.

When we consciously decide to forgive, it may take several days or longer for our emotions to catch up and to accept what the mind chose to do. This brings up the reality of human relations that go horribly wrong. When people are brutally victimized, physically or verbally abused, emotions can be severely damaged. When forgiveness seems to be out of the question, a pre-forgiveness prayer might be helpful and goes like this:

O God, I can't do it. I will not forgive _____. I'm not even sure what to do next. Help me through this. Help me sleep at night. Help me cope. Someday help me to be willing to be willing to forgive… probably not today or tomorrow, but maybe someday. Amen.

This is Step One in the forgiveness process, recognizing and identifying the hurtful reality. By frequently and sincerely praying this way, with the passage of time, it is possible (although difficult) to move on to Steps Two and Three.

All of the world's major religions have forgiveness components. However, the Jesus way of forgiveness is unparalleled by comparison. In the teachings of Jesus we have a paradigm shift. "Paradigm" comes from the Latin "paradigma," meaning to show, point out something different by example, comparison, pattern, or model. Here is a sampling as translated in the New Revised Standard Version of the Bible.

Matthew 5:38-39: "Yes, you have heard that it was said, 'An eye for an eye and a tooth for a tooth.' But I say to you, do not resist an evildoer. If anyone strikes you on the right cheek, turn the other also."

Matthew 5:43-44: "Yes, you have heard it said, 'You shall love your neighbor and hate your enemies,' but I say love your enemies and pray for those who persecute you."

Matthew 18:21-22: "Peter came to Jesus with a question: 'Lord, if another member of the church sins against me, how often should I forgive? As many as seven times?' Jesus said to Peter, 'Yes, I know that some teach that, but I say to you not seven times, rather seventy times seven.'"

As Jesus hung on the cross suffering unbearable pain and agony, he could have thought, *I have every right to die with hatred in my heart toward those who made a mockery of my trial and are now crucifying me.* No, that was not the Jesus way. His dying words as recorded in Luke 23:34, "Father, forgive them, for they do not know what they are doing." To paraphrase the forgiveness teachings of Jesus I can imagine him saying to those of us who are hurt by other people, "Yes, I understand your painful situation. But, there are ways to break out of your unhealthy, unforgiving bitterness and unacceptable behavior patterns. Try my way in getting unstuck from your hurtful past."

Maintaining and promoting healthy human relationships is an ongoing challenge. This comment by Harold S. Kushner helps us keep this in perspective.

> "If we cannot love imperfect people, if we cannot forgive them for their exasperating faults, we will condemn ourselves to a life of loneliness, because imperfect people are the only kind we will ever find."[65]

For those readers who might welcome further guidelines on entering into the process of forgiveness, here are two patterns for private prayer.

A FORGIVENESS MEDITATION[66]

In the quiet of your room or your favorite devotional spot, take some unhurried time to ponder these thoughts when someone hurts you or fails to meet your expectations.

Am I able to forgive without harboring a grudge and without frequently rehearsing the grievance in my mind? If the answer is no, what are some of the ways my resentment is working itself into my life and into my attitude?

(Pause)

How do I feel about that person?

How do I feel about myself?

(Do not rush)

Next I expand my forgiveness horizon by making a list of all the persons in my life who are difficult to be around, those who have been unkind to me, who seem to go out of their way to hurt me,

who always insist on their own way,

who do not listen to me,

who constantly try to change me,

who put me down, intimidate, and make fun of me.

(Pause)

Do I need to forgive myself by accepting God's forgiveness?

What about my relationship with God?

Am I upset or angry with God?

Do I feel that God has let me down?

(Pause)

Forgiving God, I ask you to forgive me and to cleanse me of all resentment and hurt feelings. May your love and grace flow in me and through me to others. Fill me with your peace and joy.

(Pause)

Now I return to my list of persons who have hurt and caused me pain. I lift up each one, by name, into the healing, forgiving Christ. I intentionally forgive each one, just as I have been forgiven.

(Do not rush)

Thank you, understanding and merciful God. Help me to remember this special time we have had. Bring me back here when needed. In your Holy Name...Amen!

PRAYER FOR COPING WITH PERSONAL UNFORGIVENESS[67]

Forgiving and merciful God, I want to be honest with you right now. I know I am helpless without your help in being a forgiving person every time forgiveness is called for. Even though I am so grateful for your blessings of compassion and pardon for me whenever I mess up my life, there are times when I find it totally impossible to forgive people who mess up my life.

(Pause)

Today I am dealing with a particular, complicated, personal situation (describe the details, taking as much time as you need). Yes, I know in my head I need to forgive and move on, but in my heart I am hurting and without your help I'm stuck. I guess I'm tired of living with the negative consequences of my prideful attitude and damaged emotions. I'm unsure what needs to be done next or if I'm even willing to try. Therefore, only by your grace, your wisdom, your love, and the empowering presence of your Holy Spirit can forgiveness happen in my heart, my head, my words, my actions, and in my life. Thank you, understanding God, for listening to my plight and plea. Now I will quiet myself and listen to you.

(Do not rush)

As I continue seeking your help, give me the courage to face up to my difficult personal issues with other persons and to let the Jesus way of forgiveness be my model, my teacher, my way. In His Name I pray with genuine thankfulness. Amen.

QUESTIONS TO PONDER

1. Can you recall a time in your life when you were "dumb as a buffalo" in withholding forgiveness or not accepting forgiveness from someone else?

2. Lay one of your unforgiving/forgiving situations on the grid of Doris Donnelly's three-step process. How did you do with it? Is this something you might want to keep in mind for future situations?

3. What are your thoughts on the Jesus way of forgiveness?

4. What does this wisdom from Henry Nouwen say to you?

"Forgiveness is the name of love practiced among people who love poorly. The hard truth is that all of us love poorly. We do not even know what we are doing when we hurt others. We need to forgive and be forgiven every day, every hour unceasingly. That is the great work of love among the fellowship of the weak that is the human family."[68]

Chapter 13

COPING WITH GRIEF

"What we once enjoyed and deeply loved we can never lose, for all that we love deeply becomes part of us."
—Helen Keller

Question: My husband and I were married fifty wonderful years. He died five years ago and I am still grieving. Does grief ever go away?

Reflection: A story is told about Walt Whitman (American poet and a shrewd observer of human behavior) when he was attending a funeral one day. Just ahead of him a teenage girl was standing before the open casket, staring as though she were frozen. Walt Whitman gently put his hand on her shoulder and whispered, "You don't understand that, do you?" She replied, "No, I really don't." "Well," he said, "neither do I."

Even though humankind has a 100 percent mortality rate, a universally acknowledged fact of life, the presence of death leaves us unprepared with deep feelings of loss, unrest, loneliness, sadness, and sometimes guilt and anger. Various emotions begin to surface along with unanswerable questions. Death of a loved one is always an interruption. Suddenly everything changes. We are forced to take a hard look at the uncertainties of life. What we thought was most important gets reevaluated. And immediately without an invitation comes a new experience called "grief." Coping with the reality of grief is the focus of this chapter.

To begin I would like to share with you my personal experiences with death and grief. During the past fifty-plus years as minister/pastor, I have presided at hundreds of funerals and memorial services. Never did I engage in this ministry without considerable thought, preparation, and fervent prayer for the Holy Spirit's guidance. Every time I stepped into a funeral home I was reminded of my own mortality. I recall one year during the month of March when I conducted four funerals in one week. My wife stopped answering the telephone, thinking it was most likely the funeral director wanting the pastor.

I was only six years old when my father and mother divorced. After he left our home I had very little contact with him, and consequently not many memories. I do recall attending his funeral when I was in grade school. Since he and I were never close or spent much time together, I felt no grief. After retiring many years later, I returned to my boyhood town and found the cemetery and location where my father is buried. His name is recorded in the cemetery office, but there is no headstone. With a heavy sadness in my heart, I returned home.

My first memorable experience with grief came after graduating from college. I had entered the United States Air Force for a three-year commitment. In 1958, the Air Base chaplain called to say that my father-in-law, the Rev. Lorin Stine, had been tragically killed in an auto accident. My wife, Mary Lou, was the only child in her family. Immediately we packed up, and with our one-year-old daughter left

Kansas City, Missouri, and drove to Dayton, Ohio, to be with her mother. Mary Lou's father was the senior pastor of a large congregation. Visitation the day before the funeral went on and on for several hours as hundreds of parishioners and family friends waited in line to offer a word of condolence to my wife and mother-in-law.

As you can imagine, the next day the sanctuary of the church was packed, with the overflow ushered to the Fellowship Hall to listen over the sound system. This was the first funeral I had ever attended for a person with whom I was deeply connected. Tears freely flowed among the sorrowful congregation. This senseless, unexplained tragic accident also took the lives of two other ministers in the same car. As I sat in the pew trying to listen and absorb what the speakers were saying, a strange, calming sensation came over me. I can only describe it as a very real and unexplained peacefulness in the midst of my grief. This stayed with me for several days as Mary Lou, her mother, and I adjusted to the reality of Rev. Stine's death and made plans to move forward. My mother-in-law shared with our family many years later that she did not have a good night's sleep for five years following that tragedy. Looking back on my feelings at that funeral, I am convinced I experienced the peace of God that is beyond human understanding or explaining.

After completing my Air Force duties, we moved to Dayton, where I enrolled in United Theological Seminary. At a very early age, I had felt a call to ministry and decided this was the time to explore that career possibility. Three years later in 1962, I was ordained. Ironically, the last church I served at the end of my active ministry was the same church where my father-in-law had served as pastor, Fairview United Methodist Church in Dayton. It was there, in 1995, that grief returned to our family when I conducted the funeral service for Freda Stine, my beloved mother-in-law.

After retiring in 1999, we purchased a comfortable condominium in Columbus, Ohio. The location was convenient for our children and grandchildren to visit frequently. Our winter months were spent in Fort Myers, Florida, home of my mother, Lillian Wagner, and my brother, Lynn. Longevity runs in our family on my mother's side. Her mother lived to be 103 and her grandmother was 99 when she died. Mother made it to age 97. I had the honor of presiding at her funeral, a celebration of a life well lived. Mother was a lifelong Christian, very active in her church, and read her Bible and prayed every day, as long as I can remember. When I read this verse of scripture, everyone in attendance knew it was very appropriate. The Apostle Paul wrote, "So we grieve, but not as those grieve who have no hope. For since we believe that Jesus died and rose again, even so through Jesus, God will bring with him those who have died" (I Thessalonians 4:13-14 NRSV).

In 2014, at age 79, my dear wife Mary Lou succumbed to a stroke complicated by liver disease. Our three adult children and I were with her when she died, sharing with each other a kind of grief we had never known until then. Mary Lou and I dated four years in college, followed by 58 years of faithful marriage. With a deepening love for each other, together we dealt with the uncertainties and challenges of life. Her memorial service was held in the sanctuary of the church I had served as pastor in the 1970s, the Columbia Heights United Methodist Church in Galloway, Ohio (suburb of Columbus). Over 300 were in attendance on All Saints Day, November 1st. Because participation in the Sacrament of Holy Communion was always a special time of worship for Mary Lou, we included Holy Communion in the memorial liturgy, with an open invitation for all to come to the Lord's Table. I sat on the front row holding hands with my family. Tears of thanksgiving flowed as we observed the congregation coming forward for the Bread and Cup. Yes, we grieved, but not as those grieve who have no hope.

That December I drove to the Gethsemani Abbey in Kentucky for a private retreat to think, to pray, to meditate, to cope with my grief. In January, I started attending the monthly meeting of a grief support group. This was led by the chaplain of the hospice agency that took care of Mary Lou during her last weeks. I am very thankful for hospice, truly a God-sent blessing. Participating in the grief support group proved to be most helpful as I came to realize that no two human beings grieve the same way. There are no rules, no correct ways to live with the loss of a loved one. I learned that grief never goes away and can express itself at unexpected times, called "grief bursts." Throughout her life, Mary Lou directed church choirs. Several months after the memorial service I was listening to the radio and suddenly I heard one of Mary Lou's favorite anthems: "River in Judea." Waves of grief-filled memories flooded over me and touched my soul.

Presently I am experiencing a new chapter in my life. I have moved on. I sold the condo and now live in a retirement center. Do I still miss Mary Lou? Of course. Do I still think about her? Yes, every day. My grief continues, but in a different way. Those "grief bursts" still come and go. When interacting with my family, I encourage them to tell "Mary Lou stories." It would not be good to engage in a conspiracy of silence. Recalling and sharing our memories is very therapeutic. Also, I pay attention to my dreams. As in biblical times, God continues to communicate with us in our dreams. Several months after Mary Lou was gone, I had a dream about her that was so vivid and real I wrote it down as soon as I woke up.

Mary Lou and I were together in a car in a big city. We stopped for gas, and when I got out of the car, she drove off alone. I went looking for her everywhere. At last I found her sitting peacefully at home on the sofa with her mother, Freda. Some close friends were also present. Mary Lou looked at me, did not say anything, but gave me a great big smile. I burst into uncontrollable weeping and began to hug her dearly. The next thing I knew, we were all seated at a banquet table loaded with all sorts of wonderful food. Then I woke up.

I share this with you simply to say that since that dream, I have been at peace and more settled about losing Mary Lou. Also, I do believe that she is at peace and doing okay in her new life with her beloved parents and friends. Since that night I have had several more positive dream experiences that centered on Mary Lou.

As my friend Flora Wuellner writes in her excellent book *Beyond Death*:

"I do not believe God ever intended for bodily death to be a total separation. It is a grief, an immeasurable loss when the body of our loved one dies. We cannot minimize nor trivialize that anguished sense of loss, knowing we will no longer hear the voice, the laughter, the footsteps. But we are so much more than our bodily selves. Our deep souls need never be separated. Our love and thoughts can still flow to one another and mingle. All dimensions of heaven and earth are held alive within the heart of God, who is 'God not of the dead, but of the living'" (Mark 12:27 NRSV).[69]

The emotions of grief can take up residence within us whenever we lose anything important to us. I have centered on loss of loved ones, but we can also grieve over losing our health, our job, our home, our financial resources, our friends, our pets, or any highly prized personal possession. The list is endless and the grief is real. One of my long-time mentors is Granger Westberg, a Lutheran minister who has researched the impact of grief on our health. His studies show that approximately 50 percent of patients in hospitals for physical reasons have an unresolved grief event in their past. Grief can impact physical, mental, and spiritual well-being. In his little book titled *Good Grief*, Westberg writes about ten stages of grief that he describes as a constructive approach to the challenges of loss.[70]

Stage one: We are in a state of shock.

Stage two: We express emotions.

Stage three: We feel depressed and very lonely.

Stage four: We may experience physical symptoms of distress.

Stage five: We may become panicky.

Stage six: We may feel a sense of guilt about the loss.

Stage seven: We may be filled with hostility and resentment.

Stage eight: We may be unable to return to usual activities.

Stage nine: We may experience hope gradually.

Stage ten: We struggle to affirm reality and move on.

In Westberg's workshops, I recall him saying that these ten stages can overlap and are not necessarily in a strict order. One of his main teachings is that the worst thing that can happen to a grieving person is to get stuck and not move forward in life.

One of my condo neighbors, a grieving widower, withdrew from life after his wife died. When I would visit him, it mattered not how our conversation began or on what topic, he would only talk about his departed spouse. He could not bring himself to sell her car or dispose of her belongings. All of my efforts in offering him some new experiences were rebuffed. I noticed he was losing weight, not looking well, and drinking lots of beer. He had decided to stay "stuck" in his unhealthy grief mode.

Perhaps the one word I have found that offers a positive approach to the reality of grief is coping...the opposite of denying or ignoring or getting stuck. If you are coping with your grief, you are proactive, looking for ways to move forward in the midst of personal loss. A woman asked a psychologist, "What is grief?" He said, "Grief is the expression of love, and when you grieve you allow yourself to love again." "But how do you grieve?" she asked. He replied, "You honor and celebrate your loved one's life by living your life fully." This is wise counsel. My experience is that those who do not desire to be stuck in their grief will seek out and be open to those whom they trust and who are ready to listen and assist.

Although it may not feel like it, grief is a gift from God, given to help us work through life's tragedies and losses. Grief can be good for us. I would even say that grief is a well-intended expression of God's grace. Grieving is a natural way of coming to accept that someone we love is gone and will not return. Grieving is a natural way to let go of life as we once knew it so we can hold on to what will never leave us. From James Miller's writings: "Grieving is as natural as nature itself: as natural as summer being cropped by autumn, and autumn slipping into winter, and winter awakening into spring, and spring blossoming into summer again. But grieving is more than nature's way. It is the way of nature's Grand Designer, the One behind all that is and all that shall be, the One who upholds you and all those you love, including that person who is gone but with you still."[71]

In my personal grieving, I often turn to the Holy Bible. There within its pages grief is dramatically expressed and triumphantly resolved. For instance these passages from the Book of Psalms hardly need interpretation.

"Be gracious to me, O Lord, for I am in distress; my eyes waste away from grief, my soul and body also. For my life is spent with sorrow, and my years with sighing; my strength fails because of my misery, and my bones waste away" (Psalm 31:9-10 NRSV).

"The Lord is my shepherd, I shall not want... Even though I walk through the valley of the shadow of death, I fear no evil; for you are with me; your rod and staff comfort me" (Psalm 23:1,4 NRSV).

"For you have delivered my soul from death, my eyes from tears, my feet from stumbling. I walk before the Lord in the land of the living. I kept my faith, even when I said, 'I am greatly afflicted'" (Psalm 116:8-10 NRSV).

In the Gospel of John 11:1-44 is the account of neighbors who came to console Mary and Martha as they grieved over the death of their brother Lazarus, a good friend of Jesus. When Jesus arrived to comfort the family it simply says, "Jesus wept." That short sentence tells us volumes about the human emotions of Jesus. Through the centuries Christians have interpreted Isaiah 53:3 KJV, as referring to Jesus, "He was despised and rejected...a man of sorrow and acquainted with grief." Disappointment and misunderstanding followed Jesus throughout his brief public ministry, all the way to his crucifixion. Jesus truly was a man of sorrow and acquainted with grief. Yet his teachings reveal more to life than meets the eye at any given moment or that causes our eyes to weep. What a blessing and comfort is this verse from Jesus' Sermon on the Mount, "Blessed are those who mourn (grieve) for they shall be comforted" (Matthew 5:4 NRSV).

All of us who take the risk of loving someone are candidates for grief. May we not get "stuck" in the process, but rather accept the rewarding task of coping, giving thanks for all that has been and for all that will be saying "yes."

QUESTIONS TO PONDER

1. Reflecting on your personal grief experiences, what things were beneficial? What things were less than positive?

2. Have you attempted to help a grieving person cope? If so, how did it go?

3. How do you respond to Granger Westberg's theory that 50 percent of patients hospitalized for physical reasons have an unresolved grief event in their lives?

4. What thoughts come to mind when you reflect on this statement by Joan Chittister?

5. "Death is only the birth canal to new life, the process by which we are expelled out of the womb of the world and into the womb of God, out of life lived in darkness into life lived in light."[72]

Chapter 14

THE SACRAMENT OF LAUGHTER

"For everything there is a season, and a time for every matter under heaven…time to weep and a time to laugh, a time to mourn and a time to dance."
(Ecclesiastes 3:1,4 CEB)

Question: I'm getting up in years, some of my body parts don't work too well, my memory has slipped, and because of all the bad stuff going on in the world, my sense of humor seems to be fading. I'm starting to wonder: is it okay to have a laugh or two now and then?

Reflection: Here is the short answer to your wondering. You don't stop laughing when you grow old. You grow old when you stop laughing. In my advancing years I find much truth in this verse from the Book of Proverbs 17:22 NRSV: "A cheerful heart is a good medicine, but a downcast spirit dries up the bones."

Perhaps this report from interviews at a retirement center will put a smile on your face.

Q: Why don't retirees mind being called seniors?
A: Because the term comes with a 10 percent discount.

Q: What is the biggest advantage of going back to school after you retire?
A: If you cut classes nobody calls your parents.

Q: Among retirees what is considered formal wear?
A: Tied shoe strings.

Q: How many retirees does it take to change a lightbulb?
A: Only one, but it might take all day.

Q: When is a retiree's bedtime?
A: About two hours after he falls asleep on the couch.

Q: What do retirees call a long lunch?
A: Normal.

Q: How do you prevent sagging on your face?
A: Just keep on eating until the wrinkles fill out.

After recording these questions and answers, the researcher was given this prayer by a retiree:

"O God, grant me the serenity to forget the people I never liked, the good fortune to run into the ones I do like, and please give me the eyesight to tell the difference. Amen."

The word "humor" is derived from the Old English "humour" and has a variety of meanings. When we use this word as a noun, we are indicating something as being funny, comical, or amusing. Humor is usually accompanied by smiles, laughter, and good feelings. Charles

Schultz, the "Peanuts" cartoonist, was once asked, "Can humor and faith go together?" His reply, "It's almost a necessity. Humor is proof-positive of faith, proof that everything is going to be all right with God no matter what." And we could add to Schultz's comments. Those people who find no humor in everyday living are probably those who worry too much, take themselves far too seriously, are unable to laugh at themselves, and whose attitude is heavily influenced by newspaper headlines and TV newscasts. I say this not to advocate a "head in the sand" approach to what's happening when and where. We do need a certain amount of information to survive and to be informed. A friend of mine told me one day that he stopped taking the daily delivery of the newspaper but did subscribe to the Sunday edition; that way he was only depressed one day out of seven.

In recent years scientific evidence confirms the direct relationship between hilarity and healing. It was the author Norman Cousins who got this ball rolling when he attributed his recovery to health by way of his sense of humor and the therapy of laughter. Carl Reiner, a comedic icon for more than 70 years, believes humor has enriched his life and boosted his longevity. The experts who study the effects of humor say it may be easier to laugh when you are feeling well, but it also eases stress and helps to cope with sickness and pain. They point out that laughter is beneficial psychologically and physiologically. The best part: Laughter is free and has no bad side effects.[73]

Here is the uplifting story of the amazing Mayme Carpenter, who started writing poetry in her eighties. So many people were asking for copies, she had her poems published. After that she wrote another book titled I'm 99 and Doing Fine.

Then book number three came out: "I'm a Hundred Now, But Fine Anyhow." At age 98, Mayme decided to slow down a bit. "I always got an insurance deduction for being a safe driver. I didn't want to spoil my record this late in the game. So I stopped driving."

When she took the bus to a college reunion, the person who met her asked, "Did you come by yourself on the bus?"

"Oh, no. There were plenty of other people on the bus with me."[74]

In today's kind of world, we need a healthy sense of humor to maintain our sanity, to keep life in perspective, to lighten up. As someone wisely put it, "Don't sweat the small stuff, because it's all small stuff." A good, hearty laugh is like taking an instant vacation, a free gift of God. Most humorous stories and jokes have a surprise ending as this one about the little girl who came bursting into her grandmother's house, all excited saying, "Grandma, Grandma, I've just been to the circus. And, Grandma, if you ever go to the circus you won't want to go to church ever again." Having been closely connected to many churches all my life, I enjoy "church humor."

A pastor friend told me this parsonage story several years ago. It was his practice to get up very early on Sunday mornings without disturbing his family, go to the kitchen to put on a pot of coffee, and speak his sermon out loud. One Sunday his four-year-old daughter also got up early, unnoticed by her father. After quietly listening in the background, she came into the kitchen and said, "Daddy, is that your sermon for church today?"

"Yes, darling, it is," he smilingly replied.

"Well, Daddy, if you don't mind I think I will go to the nursery."

Then there is this impressive story about Mary Alice, the Raccoon Lady, as told by her pastor, Richard L. Morgan: She was remarkable for her age. In her 80s she was still going strong, working in her garden, busy in her church work. Once we had a work day at the church to clean out the basement, and Mary Alice outworked us all. When a stranger stopped by and watched us, he seemed upset to see the work being done by older people, and asked, "Where are all the young people? They should be doing this work!" Mary Alice replied, "We *are* the young people of this church."

Even adversity evoked a touch of humor from this ageless lady. One day after church she lost control of her car and drove into a tree. She was not seriously hurt, but suffered bruises and blackened eyes. She called herself the raccoon lady because of her black eyes.

Mary Alice is one of our best teachers on growing older, for she showed us how to resist a tendency to become self-preoccupied as she reached out to embrace others and the world. She had a spiritual inner beauty, an "unfading beauty of a gentle and quiet spirit" (I Peter 3:4). Mary Alice had the ability to find humor in adversity and joy in everyday life.[75]

One of my all-time favorite columnists was humorist Erma Bombeck. Someone asked her what she hoped to accomplish through her newspaper journalism. Getting serious she responded: "What I am doing is selling an antidote for all the bad news. Is humor dead? I don't think so. But you have to look for it. I believe that laughter is a stronger weapon than protest. Humor is the survival kit for the human race."

Of all God's creatures, only humankind has the capacity to laugh. Because of the multitude of benefits we enjoy through humor I have come to appreciate what I call "The Sacrament of Laughter." Why? I am convinced there is something good, something godly, and something sacred about laughter. If we take away the world's comedians and clowns, we could easily drown in our self-filled sea of pompous superiority, arrogant attitudes, and a "me first" lifestyle. Remember comedian Red Skelton? When this authentic human being signed off his TV program, he always said, "If this hour together has brought any one of you a moment of pleasure, then we have succeeded in bringing you our show. Goodbye and God bless!"

The Sacrament of Laughter blesses, heals, and brings rays of sunshine to lighten our lives. This verse from the Book of Ecclesiastes 3:4 offers a needed balance to our everyday comings and goings, "A time to weep and a time to laugh."

From several verses in the Bible, we can say that even God has a sense of humor. In response to the kings of the earth who plot great schemes to control their world, Psalm 2:4 says, "Heaven-throned God breaks out laughing at them and is amused at their presumption" (The Message translation). For some evidence of divine humor on display: Look at a camel, a giraffe, a pelican, a kangaroo, an elephant. These oddly shaped creatures appear to have been designed by a committee that could not make up its mind. Go to any beach and observe the various human shapes and sizes strutting around with little to nearly nothing outfits. Observe odd human behavior at a garage sale, auction sale, any kind of sale, especially on the Friday after Thanksgiving. As the saying goes: "When the going gets tough, the tough go shopping."

No one would accuse God of playing practical jokes, yet God consistently does the unexpected. I think of Christmas, the birth of Jesus, who became the Christ, God's Messiah, the One whose life, death, and resurrection generated a global movement that changed the course of human history. How odd that Mary's baby was born in a smelly, dirty stable for animals. And who were the very first visitors to see the baby? Un-bathed, frightened shepherds. Then there was that unexplainable angelic choir, followed by strangers from a faraway country without names, who came bearing gifts. What a weird scenario! You would think that the designated Savior of the world could have had an upgraded birth environment with an official welcome by the government leaders and community politicians. Also, you would imagine that if Jesus was serious about getting his message to the most people in the briefest amount of time, he would have been trained with marketing and promotional skills.

Oddly enough, Jesus never traveled outside his country; he stayed close to home, and because his father was a carpenter we may assume Jesus was taught this trade. However, wherever he went, Jesus had an uncanny way of attracting large crowds by telling simple stories (parables) illustrated with familiar, everyday items: birds, weeds, mustard seed, money, wine, and bread. But here is the kicker: without a doubt, Jesus had a well-documented sense of humor in catching his hearers off guard.

When addressing the human tendency to be super critical of each other, he said, "Before you judge, before you try to remove a splinter from your neighbor's eye, I suggest you get rid of the log in your own eye." Matthew 7:15

In speaking to people of wealth, Jesus commented that it was much easier for a camel to squeeze through the eye of a needle than for a rich person to enter the Kingdom of God. The eye of the needle referred to one of the gates into the city of Jerusalem with a low header requiring people and animals to stoop down. Mark 10:23-27

Some of the show-off Pharisees would blow a trumpet before making their offering at the Jerusalem Temple. Not the best example for others. Matthew 6:1-4

Then there was the landowner hiring day laborers at different hours of the day and paying each one the same, whether he worked one hour or eight hours. This really confused those trying to make sense out of Jesus' economics, which is not the point of the story. Matthew 20:1-16

Yes, Jesus knew how to connect with his hearers. His humor and unexpected endings kept their attention. But the biggest surprise came on Easter morning. Everyone thought he was dead and buried. End of this upstart from Nazareth. But the joke's on them (the religious opposition, along with the Roman authority).

As H.A. Williams (priest and professor) tells it: "...behind their backs, without them having the slightest inkling of what is going on Jesus has popped up again like a Jack-in-the-box and is dancing about even more vigorously than before and even more compellingly. People here, there and everywhere are falling under his spell. But the brass hats and the mitered heads and stuffed shirts are facing the other way and can't see what is going on. So they continue with their dignified mutual congratulation and their serious business. But God has the last laugh with the resurrection of Jesus, the kingdom of God has drawn near." [76]

Here is the fountain of our sacramental laughter and joy. Here is the basis of our unconquerable hope. Here is the reason we can relax, laugh, and be eternally thankful for this encouraging promise of Jesus: "Be of good cheer...for I have overcome the world" (John 16:33 RSV).

I began this chapter with an emphasis on maintaining a healthy sense of humor all through life, especially in our later years. Now I close with "A Prayer As I Grow Older" by Alta Becker, Dayton, Ohio.

Lord, Thou knowest better than I know myself that I am growing older and will, someday, be old.

Keep me from getting loquacious, and particularly from the fatal habit of thinking I must say something on every subject and on every occasion. Release me from craving to try to straighten out everyone's affairs. Make me thoughtful but not moody, helpful but not bossy. With my vast store of wisdom, it seems a pity not to use it all. But Thou knowest, Lord, that I want a few friends at the end…at least enough for pallbearers, with a mourner or two. Do not let the editor head my obituary with the words "Old Crab Dies at Last…Everybody Glad." Keep my mind free from the recital of endless details. Give me wings to get to the point. Seal my lips on my aches and pains. They are increasing as the years go by. I dare not ask for grace enough to enjoy the tales of others' pains, but help me to endure them with patience. Teach me the glorious lesson that occasionally I may be mistaken. Keep me reasonably sweet. I do not want to be a saint; some of them are so hard to live with. But a sour old woman is one of the crowning works of the devil. Keep me where I can extract all possible fun out of life. There are so many funny things in life, and I don't want to miss any of it. Amen.

QUESTIONS TO PONDER

1. What role does humor play in your life?

2. Charles Schultz claims that humor and faith go together. What are your thoughts?

3. When you reflect on God's sense of humor, what examples come to mind?

4. Several teachings of Jesus are quoted in this chapter. Put yourself in the audience who first heard them. How might you have responded to Jesus?

Chapter 15

BUT WAIT, THERE'S MORE

"To know how to grow old is the master work of wisdom, one of the most difficult chapters in the great art of living."
—Henri Frederic Amiel

Question: When most of our life is spent and gone, what good things can we look forward to in our later years?

Reflection: One of my seminary classmates was a gifted artist, his specialty being sacred art. Following graduation he was employed as a full-time art illustrator for a religious book publisher. The story goes that he painted a beautiful picture, framed, ready for hanging, and gave it as a Christmas gift to a married couple, good friends from seminary days. The painting was gratefully received and looked great in their modest apartment. But, when the artist visited them, he would gaze at the painting and decide to take it home to his studio to be touched up, returning it a few days later. This giving and taking back went on for several weeks. Then one day he arrived with his painting and finally left it with them. To my readers, I confess that I went through a similar experience in writing this book. The theme or topic of each chapter was carefully selected as related to some of the questions calling for attention in our later years. But, as I read and re-read each completed chapter, without fail another. thought or idea would pop up and beg to be written into the manuscript. Finally, one day I stopped doing rewrites and decided that this last chapter would address some things not previously included. Hence the title: "But wait, there's more."

I. SPIRITUAL MATURITY

Entry into my elder years (whenever that was) should have been celebrated with cake and ice cream because everything I now experience comes under the heading: "A New Chapter Filled With Blessings Not Known Before." I am discovering that life in the fourth quarter validates Psalm 92:14 CEB, "They will bear fruit even when old and grey; they will remain vital and fresh."

"Spiritual maturity" is an interesting phrase. Could it mean that mature spirituality is an automatic experience in our older years? I think not. A better, more descriptive phrase is "spiritual readiness." When our children progress through grade school we talk about reading readiness and math readiness. I do believe that as we grow older the Holy Spirit prompts us to be more mindful and aware of spiritual matters than we were in our younger years. Of course we can deny or accept these promptings. I like to describe accepting my spiritual readiness as going with the flow of God's movements, keeping open to ever new learnings and appreciating life. Retirement is not the end, but a new beginning filled with blank pages waiting to be filled. Pastor Jorge Acevedo had a retired parishioner named Basil, whose self-accepted ministry was to call on every church visitor and take them a dozen homemade muffins, baked by his wife. Also, every Sunday Service he was at the door greeting and welcoming. Basil

139

began to slow down when age and illness started to take a toll on him. However, he continued to encourage and challenge his church friends to step up in the many ministries of the church. His mantra, "If you ain't dead, you ain't done."[77]

II. SECOND-HALF LIVING

Let us now turn to the question that opened this chapter: What good things can we look forward to in our later years? The answer depends on how each of us might anticipate life as we grow older. One projected image is "A womb with a view," as one of my seminary professors said. The womb-metaphor implies a safe and secure state of existence where all creature comforts are cared for and all we have to do is kick back, relax, and enjoy. We become full-time observers, with little or no participation in life. However, I invite you to consider another option: FIRST-HALF LIVING and SECOND-HALF LIVING. The noted psychiatrist Carl Jung first used these phrases to discuss stages and steps in human development. Richard Rohr in his significant book *Falling Upward* explains and expands this concept: The task of the first half of life is to create a proper container for one's life and to answer the first essential questions: "What makes me significant?" "How can I support myself?" (questions related to education, career, marriage, family, religion). The task of the second half of life is, quite simply, to discover the actual contents that this container can hold and deliver. A key question: "What is it you plan to do with your one and precious life?" In other words, the container is not an end in itself, but exists for the sake of our deeper and fuller life, the contents in second-half living.[78]

These two stages of life are not dependent on our chronological age. They have more to do with our mindfulness and awareness of what life, and specifically our personal life, is all about. I find it helpful to remember that we are called *human beings*, not *human doings*. Here are some comparisons:

First-Half Living	Second-Half Living
Basically in survival mode	More interested in life's values
Getting and receiving	Giving and letting go
Accumulating attachments	Practicing detachment
Caught up in the everyday details	See life in perspective
Not living fully in each moment	Appreciative of each moment
Desire to be in control	Content not to be in control
Tries to solve too many problems	Lets go of unsolvable problems
Not sensitive to physical limits	Accepts physical limitations
Chooses to fight many battles	More selective in battles
Impatience and lack of understanding	Patience and understanding
Not always attentive to those speaking	Being a more sensitive listener
Begins spiritual journey	Continues spiritual journey

Bottom line: First-half living is good and necessary. First-half living provides the foundation, the springboard to something more, called Second-half living. It seems that many people never get beyond First-half living and spend their lives repairing and trying to improve their "containers" rather than appreciating and enjoying the contents.

Esther C. Dodgen offers this perspective on Second-half living: "If we look back to the beginning of our spiritual journey, we invariably come upon moments of spiritual awakening. Sometimes these moments, which appear and reappear throughout our lives, come to us

141

while we are praying. But more often they simply rise up out of life itself. We live out our lives seeing only the tip of the iceberg, and all that does appear above the surface does so fleetingly as a brief manifestation of some unseen reality that endows the smallest of things and events with a value beyond comprehension."[79]

III. CURIOSITY and CURIOUSNESS

As long as I can remember, I have been curious about many things, motivating me to wonder, to ponder, to ask questions, to read books, to find "treasures" not always apparent. The positive results have led me to believe that curiosity is one of God's most practical and beneficial gifts. The root word "curio" from the Latin "curiosus" has several English meanings, including "inquisitive." I recall in grade school staring out the window during class and hearing the teacher say, "Jim, stop daydreaming and work on the assignment." Daydreaming, I have discovered, is not a negative habit, but can lead to new understandings. Several years later I learned some new words for curiosity, namely "serendipity/serendipitous" (the faculty or phenomenon of finding valuable or agreeable things, especially when seeking something else). When our children were young, my wife and I decided to build a modest cabin only a twenty-minute drive from our parsonage, where we could go for relaxation, recreation, peace, and quiet, plus precious family time. We named our getaway SERENDIPITY because when we went there we discovered new things and enjoyed unexpected blessings.

Serendipity is a fairly common word these days in journalism and books. Perhaps you are curious enough to wonder about the history of this interesting word. For the origin we go to a Persian fairy tale about the three princes of Serendip, who lived in the country of Serendippo and whose father was a great and powerful king. Being a good father and concerned about his sons' ability to rule the kingdom after he was gone, the king employed the best teachers to give his sons an education. However, he was not satisfied with their formal training and sent them off on a journey to complete their education. Along the way the princes accidentally discovered treasures, insights, and wisdom.[80] Many of today's scientific finds have come by way of serendipitous moments. Perhaps you have experienced some serendipity along your various pathways.

As I reflect on my life, I am amazed at the number of times I have discovered hidden treasures while trying to satisfy my curiosity. One of the recurring blessings is books. As Quaker author Elton Trueblood commented after he retired, "At home there are books to be reread and other books to be read for the first time. Here they are in my library, waiting patiently for my attention; and now, at last, I have the time. I realize that we tend to read great books too early, before we have enough experience to understand them."[81] I agree. Included on my reading list for many years are Christian devotional classics. This continuing source of information and inspiration has fostered a spiritual curiosity, causing me to appreciate the life and times of early Christians and discover more serendipity. Here is a prayer I have often prayed and recommend to you, especially during those moments when life seems lifeless, joyless, and hopeless. It just might ignite a spark of curiosity within your soul.

Gracious and Loving God, send me a surprise today, one that catches me off guard and makes me wonder. Like Easter, send me a resurrection when everything looks dead and buried. Send me light when the night seems too long. Send me a spring when the cold and frozen season seems endless. Send a new and exciting idea when my mind is empty. Send me something to do when there is nothing to do. Send me a friend when I am lonely. Send me peace when I am afraid.

Send me a future with hope. And one more thing, give me a grateful heart for all of your blessings, great and small. Amen!

IV. THE TRADITIONAL CHURCH and THE EMERGING CHURCH

Churches and congregations are noticeably changing in the 21st century, much to the chagrin of older church members. In all of the mainline churches, membership has been declining for the past several decades. High percentages of congregations average 50 or less in Sunday attendance. With the decrease in membership financial giving becomes inadequate to meet operating expenses. Consequently closing churches and selling church properties are increasingly more common. Those who grew up in churches, following WWII and during the 1950s, witnessed an unprecedented wave of new church buildings that arose to accommodate significant membership increases. Consequently these days, I have heard people comment, "Church isn't what it used to be. Looks like the church is dying. So sad."

When naming the causes for this reality, one of the major challenges is the growing number of teenagers and 20- and 30-year-olds who may claim to be spiritual but not religious. This growing demographic population is called "the nones," people who say they have no religious affiliation. These emerging adults do not want religious organizations to tell them what to do or believe. They tend to cite the golden rule as a good way to get along with people by treating others the way they want to be treated. Those who think there might be a heaven express a feeling that people go to heaven because of their good works on earth. Many of them grew up in homes where the parents had no strong religious connections, believing good parenting should allow their children to make their own decisions about spiritual matters later in life.

Church leaders today and in the days ahead have the challenge of developing creative ways to communicate with the nones. Here is an email message a friend sent to me describing how his church ministers to a younger membership:

"Our new pastor is 44 years old. He keeps his iPhone in his hands and nearby before, during, and after the worship service. He preaches from his iPad. The worship services are streamed on Facebook and over YouTube. We have four digital ways of making financial contributions. He uses DVDs to teach Bible studies. The church news, announcements, hymns and praise songs are presented on a screen during worship. We no longer print church bulletins and newsletters. You must be connected to the Internet to receive church news. Most of the congregation do not bring Bibles to church. They use their electronic devices to read the Bible. 76 million Baby Boomers and 82 million Gen Xers/Millennials live in the United States. All of them use and depend on their electronics for everything. Our church has moved into the digital age."[82]

Granted, churches may not be like they used to be; however, Christianity is not dying. God is still calling women and men to careers in Christian ministry, as evidenced by seminary enrollments. What has changed are the new ways that the Christian Gospel is being presented, as well as innovative models for congregational life in the 21st century. From the Day of Pentecost (Acts 2:1-47) when the church was birthed, the Spirit of the Risen Christ has been forming and reforming the church. The missionary journeys of the Apostle Paul launched Christianity on a global track. New churches arose adapting to different cultures and challenging situations. "Change or die" was and is the name of the game. In her book *The Great Emergence: How Christianity Is Changing And Why*, author and church historian Phyllis Tickle states that approximately every 500 years, the Church cleans out its attic and has a rummage sale, shedding ineffective traditions and cultivating new ways of presenting and living the Gospel of Jesus Christ.[83]

To highlight her observations, we go back 500 years from the 21st century and land in the 16th century specifically on October 31, 1517, when the Roman Catholic priest Martin Luther nailed his 95 theses on the church door in Wittenberg, Germany. His goal was to discuss church reform. Luther was excommunicated and became one of the catalysts that launched the Protestant Reformation. This was followed later by a counter reformation in the Roman Catholic Church. Going back 500 more years we come to the year 1054, the time of the so-called Great Schism. This is the name of the split between the Roman Catholic Pope and the Patriarch of Eastern Orthodoxy. Without going into detail, some of the issues were the practices of Holy Communion and authority in the Church. The factions went their separate ways with each becoming major Church institutions, even as they are to this day. One more glance backward 500 years to around 540, the year Gregory the Great was born. When he became Pope in 590 the Roman Catholic Church was dying and the Roman Empire was dead, truly a chaotic time in church history. Gregory rescued and advanced Christianity with the establishment of monasteries and convents. Monks and nuns provided stabilizing leadership in what has come to be called the Dark Ages.

The obvious question: Is 21st century Christianity in the throes of another 500-year attic cleaning? Only time will tell. Although we see traditional ways of being and doing church vanishing, Christianity on Planet Earth is also reforming, revising, renewing, recreating. The Body of Christ these days is gathering in a creative assortment of venues: private homes, shopping centers, restaurants, prisons, abandoned and repurposed buildings, open-air gatherings, interactive video conferencing on the Internet, and mega-churches (just to name a few).

Wherever Christians meet, there is the church. It may be constructed and presented differently, but it still fits this description of the church by E. Stanley Jones: Herein we enter a community where we agree to differ, resolve to love, and unite to serve.

Christians need not be discouraged with the changing church scene, but rather take to heart, trust, and believe what Jesus said to Peter, "I will build my church and the gates of hell will not prevail against it" (Matthew 16:18 NRSV). We can take heart in knowing that following each 500-year shake-up, Christianity continued to grow and flourish. May this hymn be our prayer of thanksgiving with grateful hearts for the Traditional Church and for the guidance and leadership of the Holy Spirit in the Emerging Church:

God of grace and God of glory, on thy people pour thy power; crown thine ancient church's story; bring her bud to glorious flower. Grant us wisdom, grant us courage, for the facing of this hour.[84]

V. CREDO (I Believe)

A creed is a brief summary of beliefs. The Apostles' Creed, first recorded in the fourth century, has become a foundational statement of the Christian religion and is often recited as an affirmation of faith in church worship services. "Credo" is Latin for "I believe," the first words of the Apostles' Creed. Throughout this book I have stated bits and pieces of my personal creed. With the possibility of repeating myself, I am now sharing a more inclusive credo for two reasons:

1. To put in writing a summary of my personal beliefs.
2. To encourage each reader to do the same thing.

You will find this writing exercise not easy or quick, but likely to be an unhurried, thoughtful, and prayerful process. Each one of us is an unique human being, a child of God, with a variety of feelings, thoughts, experiences, and beliefs. What is your personal credo?

Baptized as an infant in the Roman Catholic Church, I attended parochial grade school, where the nuns taught my catechism class. I was confirmed, and received into the Christian faith by the presiding bishop. From that moment I have been a lifelong follower of Jesus. Looking back I have nothing but gratitude for my early Christian education in the Catholic Church, which included my first Holy Communion, singing in the children's choir, and assisting with Mass. These early experiences built a spiritual foundation on which to stand and to grow. I do believe that the grace of God was present and moving in my young life before I could read or write. I am especially thankful for my grandmothers, who modeled Jesus for me. Both were active in their churches, one a member of the Evangelical United Brethren Church and one a Roman Catholic. They took me to church with them, prayed with me, discussed the Bible, and let me know that Jesus was their very best friend. I well recall the impact of Psalm 8 on my young life when I was perhaps 11 or 12 years old. This verse came to mind one clear, star-lit, summer evening as I was lying in the grass on my back looking up at the sky, all alone: "When I look at the heavens, the work of your fingers, the moon and the stars which you have established; what are human beings that you are mindful of them, mortals that you care for them?" (Psalm 8:3-4 NRSV). I wondered, *How can God, who made all that, even know I exist? Does God really know and care about me?* The answer is yes, as I came to realize later on.

As a college student I continued to be a faithful Catholic until my senior year, when I began to raise questions and explore the tenets of the Christian religion. I was taught early on that the only true church was Roman Catholic, yet when I read and studied the four Gospels,

I discovered that Jesus never set up a church organization. His only instructions were "follow me" and "love one another as I have loved you." Then when I read John 3:16 two words made me pause. "God so loved the *world* that he gave his only son so that *everyone* who believes in him may not perish but may have eternal life." My conclusion: God created and loves all human beings, not only Christians. I also discovered that Christians of all traditions and denominations read from the same Bible. How elementary, yet how liberating in my early learning. Later as a seminary student I continued to ask faith questions and develop my personal spirituality. My seminary professors were truly authentic Christians who blessed, challenged, and inspired me. Theological courses were very affirming as I learned that theology (the study of God) is faith seeking understanding.

As I describe my call to full-time Christian ministry, it was not a dramatic moment of hearing a supernatural voice (as was the experience of Paul on the road to Damascus in Acts 9:1-9); rather, gentle nudges and suggestions by the Holy Spirit (whom I think of as God in the present tense) kept calling for my attention. I entered seminary with no specific goals, other than to be faithful to Jesus and to learn more about Christianity. I totally relate to the wise person who said, "God calls those who are unequipped and then equips those who are called." Even after retiring from being a pastor, God continues to equip me for other kinds of ministry, while my goal is still to be faithful to Jesus. Through the years, I have often been asked the question: If Jesus is the Christ, the Messiah, the specially begotten Son of God, what about those religions that do not exalt and follow Jesus? What do you say about the Muslims, Hindus, Buddhists, and all the other non-Christian religions of the world? Recognizing that all religions contain elements of spiritual truth, I would answer this way: The word "religion" comes from the Latin "religio," meaning to tie, to bind, to connect, to realign, to bring the parts together, to make whole.

Religion provides the believers a way to connect with someone or something higher and beyond themselves, to find meaning in life. For the Christian this connection is a bonding to Jesus Christ. Years ago, D.T. Niles, a Christian leader and minister in India, was asked how he shared his religion with non-Christians. To quote: "Evangelism is one beggar telling another beggar where to find bread. Jesus is the 'bread of life'; whoever comes to him shall not hunger or thirst" (John 6:35 RSV).

One day in class a seminary professor made this attention-getting claim: "There is nothing new in the New Testament of the Bible, except Jesus. The basis of all of his teachings can be found in the Old Testament, which he often reinterpreted. What makes Jesus unique is his relationship with his heavenly Father as witnessed in his life, death, and resurrection." Likewise, we can say that one's relationship with Jesus, the Christ, is the essence of Christianity. I like what a Sunday School teacher told her class of adults who were asking difficult questions about how to interpret Jesus: "Always remember that nowhere in the Bible does Jesus say, 'Explain me.' He just says, 'Follow me.'" I totally agree with the Quaker philosopher and author Elton Trueblood: "A Christian is a person who, with all the honesty of which he or she is capable, becomes convinced that the fact of Jesus Christ is the most trustworthy that he or she knows in the entire universe."[85]

Here is a brief summary of my credo.

I BELIEVE:

- The Holy Trinity is one God revealed and experienced three ways: Creator, Savior, and Holy Spirit.
- The healing, saving, forgiving presence of the Risen Christ is active today.

- Life continues after death of the physical body, when we will be reunited with our loved ones and friends.
- Not in predestination, but rather, in being endowed with a free will.
- Evil is real and needs to be taken seriously.
- Prayer is a two-way dialogue with God in all of life's happenings.
- We are comforted by God, not only for our own sake, but also to be a comfort and help to others. We are blessed to be blessings.
- As God has forgiven me, so I must be a forgiving person to others.
- Life is fragile and brief. Each day is an unrepeatable miracle, a gift from God, to be lived with thanksgiving.
- Family love is special, not to be neglected or taken for granted, but rather to be nurtured and appreciated.
- My church is an extended family where I experience tender mercy and loving kindness that I can share with others, especially those who have no church home.
- God's desire and universal plan for all human beings is summed up in these significant words of Jesus: "You shall love the Lord your God with all your heart, and with all your soul, and with all your strength, and with all your mind; and your neighbor as yourself" (Luke 10:25-27 NRSV).

Therefore, this verse is my everyday goal: "Trust in the Lord with all your heart and do not rely on your own insight. In all your ways acknowledge him and he will make straight your path" (Proverbs 3:5-6 NRSV).

Now turn once more to the opening question in this chapter: When most of our life is spent and gone, what good things can we look forward to in our later years? As we grow older, our physical limitations and diminishments do increase; however, I pass on to all readers this wise word from the long-time beloved actress Betty White: "You may not be as fast on your feet, and the image in the mirror may be a little disappointing, but if you are still functioning and not in pain, gratitude should be the name of the game." Victor Frankl, a WWII holocaust survivor, puts it this way: "Everything can be taken away from a person except one thing (the last of human freedoms), to choose one's attitude in any given set of circumstances." So, with a heart that cares for others as we care for ourselves, with eyes that see beyond everyday happenings, and a spirit in tune with the Spirit of God, good things can and do happen in our fourth quarter of life.

QUESTIONS TO PONDER

1. What do these terms mean to you: Spiritual Readiness and Spiritual Maturity

2. Review the comparison columns related to first-half living and second-half living. What could you add to either list?

3. Serendipity is not planned; it just happens. What are some of your serendipitous experiences?

4. As you reflect on the author's credo, think about your own credo. What all would you include if you wrote it down and then put it away to be read every now and then? This is a reliable indicator of your spiritual journey, past and present.

Appendix A

A SPIRITUAL AND ETHICAL WELLNESS CHECKLIST[86]

This list of 25 statements can give you a quick checkup of your spiritual and ethical health. It can also help you identify areas that could be cultivated for growth. Use this checklist as a guide for enhancing your spiritual and ethical wellness.

INSTRUCTIONS: Mark each statement in one of four ways:

DW = "I'm doing well in this area of my life."

OK = "I'm doing OK, but there's room for improvement."

NS = "I know this is an area where I definitely need strengthening."

NA = "This statement does not apply to me."

1. I try to live an ethical and moral lifestyle; however, I do not consider myself to be a spiritual or religious person.
2. I take seriously my spirituality and do believe in a Supreme, Divine Being whom I call _____.
3. I have a personal relationship with God, who is the Creator of

154

the universe and Source of love, mercy, forgiveness, justice, and grace.

4. My spiritual and ethical beliefs strengthen my sense of being forgiven and my acceptance of the gift of God's loving grace.

5. My faith and spiritual values increase my ability to love God, myself, and other people (including enemies and people I find unlovely, weird, and irregular).

6. My faith enables me to know that I am at home in the universe and that I really do belong in the family of God.

7. My spiritual values increase my hope and inner peace, along with my zest for living and my desire to serve others.

8. My beliefs help me affirm rather than put down my body and my sexuality.

9. My faith and everyday spiritual exercises help me cope constructively with my losses.

10. I have evaluated the beliefs and values I learned in childhood, reaffirming and retaining only those that still ring true to me in my adult mind and heart.

11. I have learned to honor my honest doubts, viewing them as healthy growing edges of my faith even when they disturb my nostalgic need for a security blanket.

12. My spiritual beliefs and values tend to build bridges, not barriers, between myself and those with very different understandings of God and the good life.

13. I usually practice some spiritual self-care each day in such activities as meditation, prayer, Bible study, and journal writing.

14. I am a good friend with my soul, my spiritual self, which reflects the divine light within me. I am seeking new ways to make this the unifying center of my life.

15. I often experience a sense of wonder, joy, serenity, and gratitude for God's good gifts of life.

16. I am seeking to align my life with the purposes of God for me

as I understand them.

17. My experience of God's love and forgiveness help me reach out with caring to others, including those wounded by personal tragedies and put-downs by society.

18. I regularly experience spiritual highs or moments of transcendence through a variety of non-chemical means such as prayer, music, worship, nature, and reflecting on inspiring ideas and thoughts.

19. I sometimes catch glimpses of everyday miracles in mundane happenings and in ordinary people in whom I sense extraordinary gifts.

20. I participate in a caring community of faith, such as a congregation. This provides meaningful and caring support that nurtures my continuing spiritual and ethical growth.

21. My religious beliefs and experiences foster love, hope, trust, self-esteem, joy, responsibility, inner peace, and freedom.

22. My religious beliefs and experiences help me resolve destructive feelings such as fear, guilt, prejudice, hate, despair, and childish behavior patterns.

23. I affirm that all human beings, with our many conflicts and differences, are daughters and sons of the loving God, and that each one of us is unique and of significant value in God's family.

24. I often experience God's presence in the beauty and awe-awakening wonder of the natural world.

25. I have learned how to use spiritual resources that enable me to move from painful alienation from myself, others, and God to healing and reconciliation with myself, others, and God.

This spiritual and ethical checklist is adapted from *Anchoring Your Well Being*, by Howard Clinebell, published by Upper Room Books, Nashville, TN, in 1997.

Appendix B

GROUP DISCUSSION GUIDE

1. One person could lead each meeting, or group members could take turns leading the discussions.
2. Have an open invitation to anyone interested in aging gracefully. Recommend that each group member have a copy of the study/discussion book.
3. Frequency of gathering is a group decision, with the length no less than one hour or more than two for each meeting.
4. Come to each meeting with an open mind and a loving heart, prepared to learn from one another, feeling free to express disagreements and various opinions in an atmosphere of mutual support.
5. Encourage each person to share, allowing no one to dominate discussions.
6. Focus of each meeting: "Questions to Ponder" at the end of each chapter.
7. At each meeting have the group also discuss:

   During your reading of this chapter did any insights or questions surface?

Have you been challenged to consider making any changes in your life?

8. Remember: each one in the group is "a wisdom bearer." Relax, enjoy, and have a laugh or two each time you meet.

Appendix C:

Sitting in Silence, Asking Questions, Listening[87]

1. Set aside 20 minutes when no interruptions are anticipated. Settle into a comfortable chair and thank God for sitting with you.
2. Take a few deep breaths. Breathe in through your nose and out through your open mouth five or ten times or so. Take deep breaths so that if someone else were with you, they could hear you breathing. Then close your mouth and breathe normally.
3. Observe your breathing. If it helps to focus on your breathing, count your breaths up to ten and start over as needed. Then focus on a prayer word or phrase that will assist you in letting your thinking mind slow down and come to a quiet place.
4. If you find yourself distracted by a noise, or a thought, gently return your focus to your breath or your prayer word or phrase. Remember that distractions are normal.
5. When you find your mind is quiet, ask God a question. This could be a big or small question, a current one, or one you

have been asking for a while. Then let the question sink into your heart, into your breath. As you continue to breathe, observe any emotion, image, thought, feeling that comes to you. Let yourself breathe into, pray into, soak into whatever comes to you.

6. If you find yourself engaging in vigorous thoughts or debates about the question or anything else, gently return to counting your breaths or focusing on your prayer word or phrase.

7. Continue to breathe or rest in the feeling, image, or sense that came in response to your question.

8. After a time, gently let your awareness come back to your surroundings.

9. As you finish your time of meditation, say a prayer of thanks for God's presence, for the quiet time, for questions, for feelings, for anything else.

10. Repeat this pattern each day, as needed.

By Beth Richardson
Weavings magazine, Nashville, TN
May/June/July 2015, p.45-46.

Appendix D

RETIRING FROM DRIVING

By James K. Wagner

"You what?"

"Yes, I said I have retired from driving."

"Why would you ever do that. You're relatively healthy, have a great vehicle, and only eighty-five years old."

This all too common reaction prompts me to recall my mother at age 90 handing me her car keys when she retired from driving. Now that I have joined the non-drivers club, I can identify with her decision and with the consequences that follow. I probably could have continued driving for another five years or so, except my right eye double-vision was draining my confidence behind the wheel.

Isn't our primary motivation for personal independence and freedom from depending on other people the rationale to own or lease automobiles? However, with the inevitable diminishments that accompany the aging process, all who drive their own cars must confront the question: Why and when should I retire from driving? To simply raise that issue is to ponder some negative thoughts: What would I be giving up? What would I lose? After all, isn't driving your own car the American way of life?

Like the story I heard about an elderly woman having a conversation with her hairdresser after she shuffled in with her walker.

"Just came from the doctor's office. He says my congestive heart condition is not going away, my blood count and blood pressure are off the charts, my eyesight isn't what it used to be, my osteoporosis and balance are not any better, and my hearing aids don't help much."

"Oh…I'm sorry you got such a negative report."

"Hey…it's okay. I still have my driver's license."

Do you recall that "red letter" day when you passed the test and were handed your driver's license? I do. At age 15 the licensing agency granted me a restricted permit until I turned 16, so I could ride my Whizzer motorbike to work and to school. What a gift that was. I no longer had to depend on the school bus or my parents. Then the really big day arrived when at age 16, I acquired an actual, bona fide driver's license and bought my first car: a pre-owned 1942 Chevy Coupe.

When an unobservant driver ignored a stop sign and totaled my Chevy (no personal injuries), I bought a replacement car. Then another and another and another. After getting married and raising teenage children, we were a two-car family for many years. When the children left home and retirement happened we were able to get along quite nicely with only one vehicle.

You probably remember your very first car, but what about the others?

An interesting and revealing exercise is to write down the name, model, and year of all the autos you ever owned or leased. Here is my list.

'42 Chevy Coupe	'75 Oldsmobile Toronado
'54 Chevy Sedan	'85 Mercury (small 4-door)
'64 Chevy Sedan	'95 Toyota Avalon
'75 Austin (small 4-door)	2012 Lexus Hybrid
'80 Chevy II	'38 Plymouth Sedan
'86 Chevy Van	'60 Chevy Station Wagon
2010 Toyota Van	'76 AMC Pacer
2000 Toyota Avalon	'78 Chevy Sedan
'48 Nash Rambler	'84 Buick Century
'57 Volkswagen Bug	'90 Saturn Sedan
'68 Ford (small 4-door)	2010 Prius Hybrid
'72 Ford Sedan	2014 Lincoln Hybrid

These vehicles had various lengths of stay in our family, from a few months to several years. Did I ever have an emotional attachment to any of them? Honestly, no! But I did appreciate their reliability in providing transportation any time of the day or night (although the Austin was a total lemon).

In my 70 years of driving throughout the USA (includes Hawaii and Alaska) as well as in Mexico, Canada, and Australia, I never had a major accident. Fender benders, yes. Parking and speeding tickets, a few. Comfortable and enjoyable driving experiences, too numerous to count!

As I reflected on my decision to retire from driving, the question that surfaced was similar to the question I faced in trying to decide whether or not to sell my home and move into a retirement community. If I should do this, what am I giving up? The more significant question is this: If I make this move, what am I gaining?

Some positive consequences I am enjoying in the non-drivers club.

1. No more bank payments on car loans.
2. Financial savings are significant considering auto insurance, gasoline, parking fees, tire replacements, and maintenance costs to keep a car running and road-worthy, plus other out-of-pocket expenses.
3. Snow, ice, and winter road conditions are no longer a major concern.
4. Flat tires, engine trouble, and empty gas tanks are relegated to the past.
5. Being willing to graciously accept rides from friends and family, even as I had often provided transportation when needed.
6. Peace of mind in not having to be in the driver's seat and no longer being responsible for the safety of my passengers and the other road-sharing human beings.

One of the blessings of getting older is learning to be content with what one has, rather than continually striving to get and gain more. Perhaps this wise thought by an anonymous author says it best: For all that was give thanks and for all that is yet to be say "yes."

NOTES

1. David Hilton, MD, "Ethics, World View, and Health," address to the American Public Health Association, 117th Annual Meeting, October 24, 1989, quoted in *An Adventure in Healing and Wholeness* (Nashville, TN: Upper Books,1993),11.

2. Richard L. Morgan, *No Wrinkles on the Soul* (Nashville, TN: Upper Room Books, 2002).

3. Carl Jung, *Jung and Aging* (New Orleans, LA: Spring Journal, Inc, 2014), 216.

4. John Mogabgab, "Wisdom From John," Weavings Magazine, Nashville, TN. Vol. XXX, Number 1, insert.

5. Richard Rohr, *The Divine Dance: The Trinity and Your Transformation*, 2016 copyright by Richard Rohr. Published by Whitaker House, New Kensington, PA. Used with Permission. All rights reserved. www.whitakerhouse.com. Page 163.

6. Bruce Ough, newsletter article, reprinted with permission.

7. Trevor Hudson, *Beyond Loneliness* (Nashville, TN: Upper Room Books, 2016), 27.

8. Henry J.M. Nouwen, *A Guide to Prayer for Ministers and Other Servants* (Nashville, TN: Upper Room Books, 1983), 324.

9. Article, "A Vocation In Fragments," Weavings Magazine, Nashville, TN: Vol. XXX, Number 1, page 34.

10. Parker J. Palmer, *A Guide to Prayer for All Who Walk With God* (Nashville, TN: Upper Room Books, 2013), 92.

11. Susan A. Muto, *Pathways of Spiritual Living* (Petersham, MA: St. Bede's Publications, 1984), 54.

12. Op. cit., Trevor Hudson, *Beyond Loneliness*, 13.

13. Ruth Haley Barton, *Invitation to Solitude and Silence* (Downers Grove, IL: InterVarsity Press 2004), 18.

14. James K. Wagner, *The Spiritual Heart of Your Health* (Nashville, TN: Upper Room Books, 2002), 19-20.

15. James Miller, *Finding the God You Already Know* (Nashville, TN: Abingdon Press, 2013).

16. Peter Marty, The Christian Century magazine, Chicago, IL. April 12, 2017, article on page 3.

17. To recycle Christmas cards contact: St. Jude's Ranch for Children (Recycled Card Program) 100 St. Jude's Street, Boulder City, NV 89005-1681.

18. Hymn: "What a Friend We Have in Jesus" (Nashville, TN: United Methodist Publishing House, The United Methodist Hymnal, 1989), No. 526.

19. Op. cit., *Adventure in Healing and Wholeness*, 87.

20. Richard Rohr, *Yes, And* (Cincinnati, OH: Franciscan Media, 2019), 7.

21. American Bible Society, 101 N. Independence Mall EF18, Philadelphia, PA 19106.

22. The Gideons International, PO Box 140800, Nashville, TN 37214.

23. Op. cit., Wagner, *Spiritual Heart of Your Health*, 25-26.

24. Gethsemani Abbey, 3624 Monks Road, Trappist, KY 40051.

25. Rev. Donald Bartow, Presbyterian Minister Retired, Canton, Ohio.

26. Op. cit., Richard Rohr, *The Divine Dance*, 32.

27. Josephus (37–100 AD) Jewish historian provided valuable information on first century Judaism and early Christianity. (Source: Wikipedia Internet).

28. Op. cit., The United Methodist Hymnal, "Blessed Assurance," No. 369.

29. Albert Schweitzer, *The Quest of the Historical Jesus* (Published in 1906).

30. Doyle Burbank-Williams, *The Upper Room Disciplines 2019* (Nashville, TN: Upper Room Books, 2018), 235.

31. "How Great Thou Art," Words: Stuart K. Hine, Music: Swedish folk melody/adpt. and arr. Stuart K. Hine copyright 1949, 1953 The Stuart Hine Trust CIO. All rights in the USA, its territories and possessions, except print rights administered by Capitol CMG Publishing, USA, North and Central American print rights and all Canadian and South American rights administered by The Stuart Hine Trust CIO. Rest of the world rights administered by Integrity Music Europe. All rights reserved. Used by permission.

32. Tony Jones, *Did God Kill Jesus?* (New York: HarperCollins Publishers, 2015).

33. Richard Rohr, *Everything Belongs* (New York: Crossroad Publishing Company, 1999), 169.

34. Leslie Weatherhead, *The Will of God*, 1999 Abingdon Press Used by Permission. All rights reserved, 25-26.

35. Leslie Weatherhead, *A Plain Man Looks At The Cross* (Nashville. TN: Abingdon 1945), 71.

36. Randy Alcorn, *Heaven* (Carol Stream, IL: Tyndale House Publishers, 2004), xvii.

37. Elton Trueblood, *The Future of the Christian* (New York: Harper & Row Publishers 1971), 81-82.

38. Richard Rohr, *The Naked Now* (New York: Crossroad Publishing Company, 2009), 147.

39. Adam Hamilton, *Christianity and World Religions* (Nashville, TN: Abingdon Press, 2018), 144.

40. Frank J. Cunningham, *Vesper Time* (Maryknoll, NY: Orbis Books, 2017), 73.

41. Flora Wuellner, *Prayer, Stress, & Our Inner Wounds* (Nashville, TN: Upper Room Books, 1985).

42. Dale Matthews, *The Faith Factor* (New York: Viking Penguin Group, 1998), 15-16.

43. Albert E. Day, *Letters on the Healing Ministry* (Nashville, TN: Disciplined Order of Christ, 1990), 7-8.

44. Ibid., 80-81.

45. The Dalai Lama and Howard Cutler, *The Art of Happiness* (New York: Riverhead Books Penguin Group, 1998), x and 2.

46. Article in The Columbus Dispatch newspaper, Columbus, OH. 6/24/19.

47. Don Trotter quoting John Maxwell in *Caught Caring* (Meadville, PA: Christian Faith Publishing, Inc. 2018), 146.

48. Op. cit., Don Trotter quoting Flora Edwards, *Caught Caring*, 83.

49. Op. cit., The United Methodist Hymnal, "Amazing Grace," No. 378.

50. Op. cit., The United Methodist Hymnal, "Great Is Thy Faithfulness," No. 140.

51. Op. cit., John Mogabgab, "Wisdom From John," See Insert.

52. Op. cit., Richard Rohr, *Yes, And*, 78.

53. John Newton (1724–1807) British sailor & Anglican clergyman (Source: Wikipedia Internet).

54. Op. cit., Frank J. Cunningham, *Vesper Time*, 101.

55. Joan Rivers, quoted in The Columbus Dispatch newspaper, Columbus, OH. Spring 2020.

56. Adrian Van Kaam & Susan Muto, *The Power of Appreciation* (New York: Crossroad Company, 1993), 152.

57. Op. cit., Frank J. Cunningham, *Vesper Time*, 94.

58. James K. Wagner, *Blessed To Be A Blessing* (Nashville, TN: The Upper Room, 1980), 84.

59. Op. cit., Adrian Van Kaam & Susan A. Muto, *The Power of Appreciation*, 19.

60. Ibid., 20.

61. Andy Halatek, Thanksgiving Thoughts, with permission to reprint.

62. James K. Wagner, *Forgiveness: The Jesus Way* (Lima, OH: CSS Publishing Co. Inc., 2007) 32-33

63. Ibid., 42.

64. Ibid., 34.

65. Ibid., 71.

66. James K. Wagner, *An Adventure in Healing and Wholeness* (Nashville, TN: Upper Room Books, 1993), 53-54.

67. Op. cit., James K. Wagner, *Forgiveness: The Jesus Way*, 139-140.

68. James K. Wagner, *Letters To Christopher* (Bloomington, IN: WestBow Press, 2018), 48-49.

69. Flora Wuellner, *Beyond Death* (Nashville, TN: Upper Room Books, 2014), 79.

70. Granger Westberg, *Good Grief* (Philadelphia, PA: Fortress Press, 1971), see Contents page.

71. James E. Miller, *Winter Grief, Summer Grace* (Minneapolis, MN: Augsburg Fortress, 1995), 82.

72. Joan Chittister, *Illuminated Life* (Maryknoll, NY: Orbis Books, 2000), 133-134.

73. Carl Reiner, Article in The Columbus Dispatch newspaper, Columbus, OH. 7/7/19.

74. Richard L. Morgan, *Autumn Wisdom* (Nashville, TN: Upper Room Books, 1995), 25.

75. Ibid., 39.

76. Op. cit., H.A. Williams, *A Guide To Prayer For Ministers and Other Servants*, 41-42.

77. Jorge Acevedo & Wes Olds, *A Grace-Full Life*, 2017 Abingdon Press Used by permission. All rights reserved, 92.

78. Richard Rohr, *Falling Upward* (San Francisco, CA: Jossey-Bass, 2011), 1.

79. Esther C. Dodgen, *Glimpses of God Through the Ages* (Peabody, MA: Hendrickson Publisher 2003), 419.

80. The Three Princes of Serendip (Source: Wikipedia Internet).

81. Richard L. Morgan, *I Never Found That Rocking Chair* (Nashville, TN: Upper Room Books, 1992), 40.

82. John Penn, email message to James K. Wagner, 12/20/19.

83. Phyllis Tickle, *The Great Emergence* (Grand Rapids, MI: Baker Books, 2012), 19.

84. Op. cit., The United Methodist Hymnal, "God of Grace and God of Glory," No. 577.

85. Elton Trueblood, *A Place To Stand* (New York: Harper & Row Publishers, 1969), 38.

86. Appendix A: H. Clinebell, *Anchoring Your Well Being* (Nashville, TN: Upper Room Books 1997).

87. Appendix C: Beth Richardson, Weavings Magazine, Nashville, TN: M-J-J, 2015, 45-46.

Recommended Reading

Acevedo, Jorge and Wes Olds. *A Grace-Full Life*. Nashville: Abingdon Press, 2017.

Anderson, Kevin. *Now Is Where God Lives*. Monclova, OH: CLB Press, 2018.

Alcorn, Randy. *Heaven*. Carol Stream, IL: Tyndale House Pub, 2004.

Alexander, Eben. *Proof of Heaven*. New York: Simon & Schuster, 2012.

Barton, Ruth Haley. *Invitation to Solitude and Silence*. Downers Grove, IL: InterVarsity Press, 2004.

Buchanan, Missy. *Aging Faithfully*. Nashville: Upper Room Books, 2011.

Chittister, Joan. *Illuminated Life*. Maryknoll, NY: Orbis Books, 2000

.The Gift of Years. *Katonah*, New York: BlueBridge, 2008.

Clinebell, Howard. *Anchoring Your Well Being*. Nashville: Upper Room Books,1997.

Cunningham, Frank J. *Vesper Time*. Maryknoll, New York: Orbis Books, 2017.

Donnelly, Doris. *Learning to Forgive*. Nashville: Abingdon Press, 1979.

. *Putting Forgiveness Into Practice*. Allen, Texas: Argus, 1982.

Hamilton, Adam. *Christianity and World Religions*. Nashville: Abingdon, 2019.

. *The Walk*. Nashville: Abingdon, 2019.

Hudson, Trevor, *Beyond Loneliness*. Nashville: Upper Room Books, 2016.

Job, Rueben P. and Norman Shawchuck. *A Guide to Prayer for Ministers and Other Servants*. Nashville: Upper Room Books, 1983.

.*A Guide to Prayer for All God's People*. Nashville: Upper Room Books, 1990.

.*A Guide to Prayer for All Who Seek God*. Nashville: Upper Room Books, 2003.

John S. Mogabgab. *A Guide to Prayer for All Who Walk With God*. Nashville: Upper Room Books, 2013.

Jones, Tony. *Did God Kill Jesus?* New York: HarperOne, 2015.

Kaam, Adrian Van and Susan Muto. *The Power of Appreciation*. New York: Crossroad, 1993.

Keating, Thomas. *Open Mind, Open Heart*. New York: Continuum Pub., 1992.

Long, Jeffrey and Paul Perry. *God and the Afterlife*. New York: HarperOne, 2016.

Matthews, Dale A. *The Faith Factor*. New York:Viking,1998.

Miller, James E. *Winter Grief, Summer Grace*. Minneapolis: Augsburg, 1995.

Miller, Stephen M. *The Complete Guide to the Bible*. Uhrichsville, OH: Barbour Publishing Co., 2007.

Moore, Thomas. *Ageless Soul*. New York: St. Martin's Press, 2017.

Morgan, Richard L. *Autumn Wisdom*. Nashville: Upper Room Books, 1995.

. *Fire In The Soul*. Nashville: Upper Room Books, 2000.

. *I Never Found That Rocking Chair*. Nashville: Upper Room Books, 1992.

. *No Wrinkles on the Soul*. Nashville: Upper Room Books, 1990.

Jane M. Thibault. *Pilgrimage into the Last Third of Life*.

Nashville: Upper Room Books, 2012.

Muto, Susan A. *Pathways of Spiritual Living*. Petersham, MA: St. Bede's Pub., 1884.

Rohr, Richard. *Everything Belongs*. New York: Crossroad, 1999.

. *Falling Upward*. San Francisco, CA: Jossey-Bass, 2011.

. *Immortal Diamond*. San Francisco, CA: Jossey-Bass, 2013.

. *The Divine Dance*. Kensington, PA: Whitaker House, 2016.

. *The Naked Now*. New York: Crossroad, 2009.

. *The Universal Christ*. New York: Convergent Books, 2019.

Rutledge, Fleming. *The Crucifixion*. Grand Rapids, MI: Eerdmans Pub., 2015.

Strobel, Lee. *The Case For Christ*. Grand Rapids, MI: Zondervan Pub., 1998.

. *The Case For Easter*. Grand Rapids, MI: Zondervan Pub., 2003.

Taylor, Barbara Brown. *Holy Envy*. New York: HarperCollins Pub., 2019.

The Dalai Lama and Howard C. Cutler. *The Art of Happiness*. New York: Riverhead Books, 1998.

Tickle, Phyllis. *The Great Emergence*. Grand Rapids, MI: Baker Books, 2008.

Trotter, J. Don. *Caught Caring*. Meadville, PA: Christian Faith Publishing, 2018.

Trueblood, Elton. *A Place To Stand*. New York: Harper & Row Pub., 1969.

. *The Future of the Christian*. New York: Harper & Row Pub., 1971.

Wagner, James K. *An Adventure in Healing and Wholeness*. Upper Room, 1993.

. *Anna, Jesus Loves You*. Nashville: Upper Room Books, 1985.

. *Blessed To Be A Blessing*. Nashville: Upper Room Books, 1980.

. *Forgiveness: The Jesus Way*. Lima, OH: CSS Publishing Co., 2007.

. *Healing Services*. Nashville: Abingdon Press, 2007.

. *Letters To Christopher*. Bloomington, IN: WestBow Press, 2018.

. *The Spiritual Heart of Your Health*. Nashville: Upper Room, 2002

Weatherhead, Leslie. *A Plain Man Looks At The Cross*. Nashville: Abingdon, 1945.

. *The Christian Agnostic*. Nashville: Abingdon, 1965.

. *The Will of God*. Nashville: Abingdon Press, 1995.

Westberg, Granger. *Good Grief*. Philadelphia: Fortress Press, 1973.

Wing, Richard. *Finding Your Lambarene*. First Community Church, Columbus, Ohio, 2011.

Wuellner, Flora. *Beyond Death*. Nashville: Upper Room Books, 2014.

. *Prayer, Stress, and Our Inner Wounds*. Nashville: Upper Room, Books, 1985.

Acknowledgments

A book manuscript is never the product of one person. In a fleeting moment of inspiration the concept for a book is launched in the author's mind, followed with a fledgling theme or topic, along with a beginning outline. Then come the endless hours of word processing with many rounds of writing, rewriting, and editing. Finally the manuscript arrives completed and ready for publication. As I have researched and studied the various subjects in this book, it became obvious that much of what I have written I have learned from others. I tried diligently to document the quoted texts; however, not being able to locate the sources of some quotations, I offer my sincere apologies.

To these special persons I am indebted: Laszlo Bujdoso (my personal "all things electronic" technician); Kaye Najmulski (superb proofreader); my AGOS buddies (Aging Gathering Of Souls) Tim Heaton, Gene Hulbert, Mike Pratt, John Hinton; and most of all to my fellow residents at Friendship Village Columbus, a vibrant, caring, compassionate community of wisdom bearers.